WILLIAM BECKNELL
Father of the Santa Fe Trade

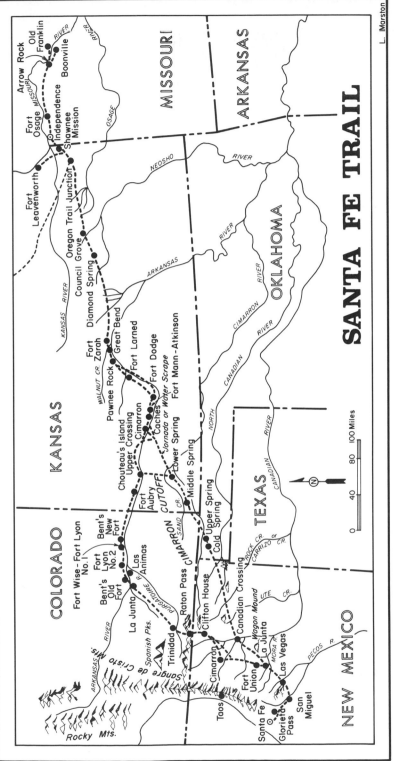

S O U T H W E S T E R N   S T U D I E S

Monograph No. 68

WILLIAM BECKNELL
Father of the Santa Fe Trade

by

Larry Bcachum

TEXAS WESTERN PRESS
The University of Texas at El Paso

Paper: isbn 0-87404-127-9   Cloth: isbn 0-87404-128-7

ABOUT THE AUTHOR

Larry Mahon Beachum was born September 21, 1948, in Dallas, Texas. What was to become an abiding interest in the culture and heritage of the American Southwest began during his childhood spent in McAllen, located in the Lower Rio Grande Valley in Texas. That interest was enhanced during his youth when he worked at his parents' cattle ranch near Maypearl, Ellis County, Texas, on weekends and during summer vacations. A 1966 graduate of Justin F. Kimball High School, Dallas, he then attended Dallas Baptist College where he earned a B.A. in Secondary Education and Social Studies in 1970. In 1979 he received an M.A. in History, with emphasis on the American Southwest, from Southern Methodist University. He has taught Texas History and American History in the Alamo Heights Independent School District in San Antonio, and currently teaches Texas History in the Waxahachie Independent School District, Waxahachie, Texas. He resides in Dallas, and has a daughter, Jenny, and a son, Andrew. Beachum reserves at least one week a year for travel to historic regions outside Texas. Recently he visited Virginia, Arizona, Wyoming and Colorado. He plans to continue research and writing about the Southwest.

WILLIAM BECKNELL
FATHER OF THE SANTA FE TRADE

Chapter I

A Fortune Made and Lost

LONG BEFORE anyone had thought of him as "Father of the Santa Fe Trade," William Becknell could look back at the age of thirty-four on a full career as an Indian trader in the lower Missouri River Valley.[1] He was born in 1787 or 1788 in the Rockfish Creek area, that part of Amherst County, Virginia, which became Nelson County in 1806.[2] His grandfather, William Becknall [sic], a veteran of the French and Indian War,[3] had settled there — on the eastern edge of the Blue Ridge Mountains southwest of Charlottesville — no later than 1762.[4] The patriarch's 1781 will listed eight children, evidently from two marriages: Samuel, William Jr., Thomas, and John by the first wife, and Micajah, Ruth, Anna, and Mary by the second.[5]

The Revolutionary War had brought danger and sacrifice to these hardy Virginians. Two of the elder Becknell's neighbors were Tories, and had lost their farms for their loyalty to the Crown, but the Becknells paid a much higher price for embracing the cause of American independence: two of Thomas Becknell's sons, James and Thomas, died in 1777 serving in Daniel Morgan's Sixth Virginia Regiment of Foot in the campaign against Burgoyne's offensive in New York.[6] Micajah Becknell also served in the Continental Army in the closing months of the conflict, his father's statement that "times are troublesome and he may be taken to the Wars" having proved prophetic.[7]

Micajah was spared the fate of his far-ranging kinsmen, however, and returned to Amherst County to wed Pheby Landrum on October 23, 1782.[8] It was to this couple that William Becknell was born some five years later.[9]

[1]

The details of young William's childhood are lost, but images of a log cabin home in the shadow of the rolling Blue Ridge, barefoot freedom offset by new responsibilities, and infrequent encounters with the mysteries of rustic education spring readily to mind. The rudiments of frontier democracy were evidently not denied him, for Micajah Becknell voted regularly. But the American frontier had not lingered in melancholy mountain shadows, nor had it stalled on the eastern bank of the turbid Mississippi River. In 1798, for example, pioneers as diverse as woodsman Daniel Boone and merchant Moses Austin settled in that part of Spanish Louisiana to be known as Missouri.[10] These precursors were soon followed by others of their kind.

In 1803 the United States purchased the vast Louisiana Territory. Four years later,[11] Becknell married Jane Trusler in Amherst County, but did not long delay his appearance on the Louisiana frontier. We can be fairly sure that, by 1810, he was in the St. Louis Area.[12]

The lower Missouri River Valley offered much to the pioneer of 1810. The region's population of 20,845 had doubled in the seven years since the great purchase, the increase was due mainly to Anglo-American immigration. St. Louis, founded in 1764, was an essential township and headquarters for the western fur trade. West of St. Louis, across the Missouri River, was St. Charles, founded in 1780, a village of about 100 families in 1803. Other settlements were scattered southward along the Mississippi River. Under the French and Spanish regimes, early explorers had discovered lead and salt deposits in the countryside, and the rich soil along the Mississippi and Missouri rivers and their tributaries promised bountiful harvests to those who could cultivate it. The rivers also provided natural highways that stimulated trade and facilitated the influx of Anglo-American settlers.

The Ohio River offered access from the east; the Mississippi, which defined Missouri's eastern boundary, was the main commercial artery of the West; and the Missouri flowed from Montana and the plains through the heart of the Territory.

These natural highways combined to make Missouri attractive to settlers and a logical base of operations for the exploration and exploitation of the American West.[13]

William Becknell's participation in the opening of the West began on a modest if ironic note. He first settled at Gatty's Emplacement, a half mile west of St. Charles, where he served on a jury in November, 1811. He then went to work for James and Jesse Morrison, brothers of entrepreneur William Morrison of Kaskaskia. It was on their behalf that Becknell delivered a horse and gun to Robert McKnight in April, 1812, in the Boone's Lick region of central Missouri, as McKnight's ill-fated party carried out a vain attempt to open Spanish New Mexico to trade with the United States.[14] Any seeds sown on that occasion would lie dormant for nine eventful years on the Missouri frontier.

Missouri was far from subdued. Numerous Indian tribes inhabited the region, among them Shawnees, Delawares, Missouris, Osages, Sacs, and Foxes. The Shawnees and Delawares had been partially subjugated during the Spanish regime, while the Missouris were dispersed by the Sacs and Foxes who held sway north of the Missouri River as far as present-day Iowa. The lands south of the Missouri, chiefly along the Osage River, were held by the formidable Osage. The influx of Anglo-American settlers into tribal lands was ominous, for Indians there, as elsewhere, resented the newcomers' encroachment, while settlers nurtured a generations-old distrust of Indians. Their uneasy coexistence in Missouri disintegrated after the outbreak of war between Great Britain and the United States in 1812 — a war which would involve William Becknell.

Great Britain had long been influential among the Indians of the upper Mississippi valley and the area south of the Great Lakes. Competition with the United States for the fur trade was on a continent-wide scale; the reduction of the American settlement around the confluence of the Ohio, Mississippi, and Missouri rivers would be a major military and economic victory. British agents on the frontier procured a widely deployed army of allies among various tribes of the upper Mississippi basin; this was a portent of bloodshed in the Missouri settlements.

Although the white population had doubled in Missouri since 1803, the area of settlement had not expanded greatly beyond the confines of earlier French and Spanish colonization. Log blockhouses had been constructed in the advanced areas of Anglo-American settlement; however, isolated farms and lonely trails connecting them typified the vulnerability of the settlers. The headwaters of the Illinois River were the bailiwick of British agents, but British influence was greater east of the river than in Missouri. The situation seemed critical, nevertheless, because the United States government was ill-prepared to defend the area.[15]

> The defense of Missouri was left largely to its own citizens throughout the war. There were only 241 men of the regular army stationed west of the Mississippi on June 6, 1812, and their number was not materially increased until after the war.

> After considerable urging from Missouri and Illinois congressmen, Congress graciously authorized the territories to raise companies of rangers for their own defense. The rangers equipped themselves with provisions, clothing, horses, rifles, and ammunition. The United States paid the rangers 75¢ a day for service on foot, $1.00 a day for mounted service — as late as 1815 for the performance of duty in 1812.[16]

William Becknell would serve two adventurous years as a mounted ranger in units commanded by members of the family of Daniel Boone. Because this association is instrumental in tracing Becknell's wartime experiences and influenced his post-war activities, a synopsis of the Boone family offers insight.

Daniel Boone's oldest surviving son, Daniel Morgan Boone, immigrated from Kentucky to Femme Osage Creek in the District of St. Charles in 1796, and the elderly woodsman followed him the next year. By 1803, youngest son Nathan and daughter Jemina Boone Callaway and her husband, Flanders, also resided in the district.[17] Nathan and Daniel Morgan Boone soon plied their wilderness skills far up the Missouri River, operating a salt works in central Missouri as early as 1805.[18] Their nephew, James Callaway, was paymaster for the expedition that ascended the Missouri to construct Fort Osage, near present-day Kansas City, in 1808, under the guidance of Daniel Morgan Boone.[19] The Boone brothers and their nephews were in the vanguard of Missouri's defense activities during the War of 1812.

William Becknell joined Captain Daniel Boone's company of United States Mounted Rangers, part of Colonel William Russell's regiment, at St. Charles, with the rank of First Sergeant on May 19, 1813.[20] Boone's company spent the following year building forts and patrolling in a defensive arc northwest of St. Charles between the Mississippi and Missouri Rivers.

Rumors of a hostile Indian force massing in the northern Mississippi River basin resulted in the company's initial assignment in June, 1813: the construction of a small fort on the Mississippi eight miles above the mouth of the Cuivre River. The outpost was called Cap au Gris after a sandstone bluff of that name across the river.[21] Construction at Cap au Gris may have been partially supervised by Lieutenant James Callaway, scion of the Boone family, who joined the company "in early summer," and took pride in his fort building abilities.[22]

Becknell and his fellow rangers were sent to the upper Cuivre River country in July. He may have joined Callaway in a perilous recon- naissance of the upper Illinois River by a picked force of sixteen or seven- teen rangers commanded by Captain Nathan Boone in August.[23] Becknell was present at "Camp Upper Cuivir [*sic*]" on August 31, and evidently spent the following two months there.[24] That Callaway spent the same period in General Benjamin Howard's expedition against Peoria[25] further clouds the question, but it is certain that First Sergeant William Becknell was active in the defense of Missouri during this time.

The last quarter of 1813 found Becknell, Callaway, and the rest of Daniel Morgan Boone's Rangers constructing a fort approximately fifty miles up the Missouri River from St. Charles at Loutre Island.[26] A part of the mainland during dry periods, Loutre Island was at the mouth of the Loutre River, near the western boundary of present Warren County.[27] The heavily wooded twelve-mile-long island had been settled early in the Anglo-American surge up the Missouri River Valley, and, because of fre- quent Indian depredations, the government fort was planned to augment local family forts.

By late November, the rangers had suffered through foul weather and "bad camps," and but one cabin had been completed before snow fell the night of November 23. The next day, Callaway wrote his wife that "it is not as yet verry [*sic*] Comfortable but we are at work as fast as possible the fort is as far forward as Could be expected I think the men will all get in their Quarters against Sunday knight [*sic*] . . . ."[28]

The completed fort was named in honor of army officer Eli B. Clemson.[29] William Becknell remained stationed there until late April, 1814,[30] when the company was ordered down river to a blockhouse on the Mississippi near Portage des Sioux.[31]

The American situation in the Missouri and Illinois region was critical during this time. The British controlled the upper Mississippi Valley, U.S. Army troops were being withdrawn for duty in the East, Illinois Rangers' enlistments were near expiration, and each week brought more macabre reports from outposts near and far. Such was the public's dismay, that Governor William Clark of Missouri was forced to organize a 200-man ex- pedition to ascend the Mississippi and capture Prairie du Chien.[32]

Becknell and his fellow rangers at Portage de Sioux, with their enlistments to be terminated May 19, could only speculate about their future. Uninformed, they were anxious as to whether they would be mustered out of service or ordered to join Clark's expedition. Lieutenant Callaway wrote on May 1 that "we have no news about the rangers whether they will be raised or not neither Do I Know when the boats will start from St. Louis." On May 9 he noted that "I Do not expect to Come home untill my time of service expires it is now verry [sic] short and we have no Orders for Raising another Company as yet . . . ."[33]

Orders to raise a new Ranger company arrived within the next few days, Clark's expedition having ascended the river in the meantime. Becknell reenlisted as a private in Boone's company at St. Charles on May 19, 1814.[34] By June, the rangers were on duty at Stout's Fort, a small stockade some forty miles northwest of St. Charles.[35]

With no sign of hostile Indians, but news of Indian ambushes elsewhere in the Cuivre River region, the rangers kept constantly alert and "Spies and reconnitering [sic] parties" issued from the fort "in all Directions."[36]

On June 21, 1814, Daniel Morgan Boone resigned as company commander to accept a colonelcy, and Lieutenant Callaway became commanding officer.[37] Orders soon came to divide the company. Callaway dispatched Lieutenant Jonathan Riggs, one sergeant, and fifteen men with forty days' provisions to Cap au Gris where they were to join an expedition under Lieutenant John Campbell to relieve the beleaguered American garrison at Prairie du Chien. Another fifty-five rangers left Stout's Fort with enough supplies for fifteen days. Their destination and purpose are uncertain, although they were apparently not acting in conjunction with Lieutenant Riggs' detachment.[38]

William Becknell left Stout's Fort with one of these groups: He was "absent, on command" on June 30.[39] He may have participated in Campbell's disastrous expedition in which Lieutenant Riggs and the rangers fought a day-long battle from their grounded boat at Rock River, escaping destruction only by feigning death and then raking their approaching tormentors with a shower of grapeshot and rifle balls. The badly mauled expedition returned to St. Louis by July 28, six days after the battle.[40] Becknell may have taken part instead in the fifty-five-man force's activities.

That July, at any rate, was an auspicious month for William Becknell; General Benjamin Howard appointed him an Ensign, or most junior commissioned officer, on the thirteenth of the month.[41] James Callaway was promoted to Captain the same day.[42]

By August 9 the company was at "Isleand [sic] Camp opposite Cappo Grais [sic]," preparing for an expedition to recapture Prairie du Chien, which had fallen to the enemy on July 20.[43] Ensign Becknell and Captain Callaway went to General Benjamin Howard's quarters on the eve of departure, August 21, 1814. Cognizant of the dangers ahead and in debt to Callaway for $400, General Howard instructed the Captain to write a due bill and Howard signed it. Callaway showed the document to Becknell upon leaving the General's quarters.[44]

At twelve o'clock the next day, the 400-man force, commanded by Major Zachary Taylor, departed Cap au Gris "with hearts elated and sails filled." James Callaway's diary describes the expedition and its events much as William Becknell must have experienced them: days of back-breaking toil against the relentless current, an outbreak of measles among the men, a bountiful breakfast of peaches from a deserted farm, the death and burial of one of the men, broken steering oars and masts, and always the nervewracking vigil for "Indian sign."[45]

On the morning of Sunday, September 4, after an all-night voyage of fifteen miles, the expedition surprised a group of Indians in a canoe at the mouth of Rock River. Several warriors leaped ashore to spread the invasion alarm while the remainder paddled the canoe out of sight.

The flotilla continued up the Mississippi for three miles to find both shores swarming with Indians. Gathering darkness and the apparent hostility of the Indians dictated that camp be made at an island on the west side of the river. The rangers and United States Army regulars spent a blustery night aboard their pitching vessels while an Indian bonfire reflected across the water.

The Battle of Credit Island began about three hours before dawn when Indians fired on the expedition, wounding two sentinels. At daybreak Callaway's company searched the island, with two rangers wounded and one Indian killed. The Missourians returned to their boats to join the defensive deployment of the flotilla, whereupon a British battery 600 yards across the river opened fire. Three-, four-, six-pound shot churned the muddy water as boatmen tried to maneuver their craft in high winds. Captain Callaway told how the situation worsened:

> They found out their mistake and began to Lower thir [*sic*] peices [*sic*] and they stuck them in to our boats, masts, sails stering [*sic*] oars and at Last was base enough to knock the Splinters into the men's faces we Returned the fire from our swivels and small arms but found we could not hurt them owing to the Distance We Dropped Down about three miles and they fired at us all the Time with small armes [*sic*] and instead of the Horses we saw the evening before on the plains it was lined with savages armed and fireing [*sic*] at us . . . .

The current swept the battered expedition to safety and a council of officers, among them Callaway and Becknell, was called. They decided to retreat to "the lower rapids of the Mississippi" and build a fort.[46]

William Becknell and the rest of Callaway's company assisted in building the new outpost, Fort Johnson, during mid-September. The 100-foot-square enclosure, containing thirteen log buildings, was on a hill that rose 100 feet above the east bank of the Mississippi, the modern site of Warsaw, Illinois.[47] The fort was to have a short and controversial history.

Major Taylor decided to leave Callaway's company and Whitesides' Illinois Rangers to garrison the fort while the rest of the expedition returned to St. Louis.[48] Callaway wrote his wife on September 25 that "we have not more than ten Days of provisions for the Troops at this place and I am assured by Major Taylor that if Provisions does not Reach this place against the Last of this month that the post will be Evacuated and all the men Come Down."

William Becknell, granted a furlough by Lieutenant Colonel Dodge,[49] was evidently preparing to leave Fort Johnson as Callaway wrote his letter: "I have riquested [sic] Mr. Becknell to go to Genl Howard and Know of him how Long I am to Stay at this place and if I am to Stay here he will Call and see you and you will Send me Some winter cloathes [sic], sugar, Cheese, butter."[50]

The Fort Johnson garrison managed to survive without promised provisions until the third week of October, when the men decided to abandon and burn the fort. Their arrival at Cap au Gris set off a vitriolic outcry against officers of the regular army, accused of logistical incompetence that led to the debacle.[51]

Callaway's Company spent the next seven months at Fort Clemson on the Missouri River, where news of the Treaty of Ghent reached them. The treaty specified that no action could be taken against tribes allied with Britain and that treaties would be negotiated with the tribes. Six months passed before negotiations began, and the Missourians' restraint only served to embolden the Indians.[52] In the midst of the bloody spring of 1815, the rangers of Fort Clemson suffered "the most serious calamity that befel [sic] the settlers during the Indian war."[53]

Events of March 4 and 5, 1815, prefaced the disaster, and are crudely outlined by James Callaway in a letter to his wife dated March 5:

> I have Just Returned from Bests fort, on yeastearday evening
> Mr. John Wheldon and one of my men was up their and heare
> four or five Guns and saw two Indians they Returned to this

place and we marched up to Mr. Quicks in order to save them families from the Tomohwak we arrived thir after swimming wading and Treaveling Through the mud and water untill about midnight this morning we went on to Bests Fort but the rain had put out all the [Indian] sign we Returned to Camp where the Spies from Louter Creek say they saw the sign of six Horses and one footman I am Just a going to start after them.[54]

Callaway, Lieutenant Jonathan Riggs, and fourteen other men drew provisions and thundered out of Fort Clemson, leaving Ensign William Becknell in charge. March 6 passed with no alarming news, but by the evening of March 7 it was apparent to Becknell that the number of Indians afield was at least four to five times greater than had been thought.

The departure of Callaway's detachment had so depleted the garrison that Becknell doubted an Indian attack could be withstood. He wrote to Colonel William Russell, the regimental commander, recounting events of the past three days and warning that Fort Clemson was untenable. On March 8 Becknell added a chilling postscript to his report and sent it to St. Louis, where it appeared in the *Missouri Gazette* on March 18:

> Fort Clemson March 7th 1815
>
> John Wheldon and four other citizens who were on the 4th Inst. at a neighboring family fort, which was evacuated, heard several guns fired, and saw 2 indians run after the cattle they had shot, come to our camp and reported what they [had] heard and seen. Captain James Callaway with the few men he had, went in pursuit of the savages, but after a long and fatigueing march could not discover them. Late in the evening of the same day, two of our spies who were out on the Loutre creek fell on a fresh trail of eight indians on horses; these were pursued by the captain immediately after his return to camp with all the men he could collect, with four days provision. About 12 o'clock this day, John Stewart a citizen residing near Loutre creek, with whom Cap Callaway had left two men to assist him in moving into the island, were fired upon by 20 or 30 indians. Stewart was wounded in the foot, another man near the enemy escaped although their horses were so cut to pieces with the bullets as to give out.
>
> John Manley who set out for Boons Lick has been killed by these Indians. My force here being small, I have notified some of the inhabitants to join me as I am unable to stand an assault.

March 8th

Captain Callaway was defeated and killed last night about sunset. He fell in with the party above mentioned. The savages lay in ambush — five men are missing and two wounded. I have given the alarm along the frontier.[55]

Callaway had found the stolen horses at about two o'clock on the afternoon of March 7, and after dispersing a group of squaws guarding the animals, decided to retrace his trail to Fort Clemson. Riggs warned that this would invite ambush, but Callaway discounted the advice, and was sufficiently confident to order a halt to rest horses and prepare food later in the afternoon. The captured horses were entrusted to three men in the advance of the column when travel resumed. As the three urged their charges across rain-swollen Prairie Fork, near Loutre Creek, Indians on both sides of the stream op-ened fire, cutting down all three rangers after they had reached the far bank. Calloway followed and his horse was shot from under him. He ran along the bank as the Indians closed in, then dived into the water where he was shot in the head while attempting to swim to safety.

The surviving members of the detachment followed a circuitous route back to the fort. A party of men, Becknell perhaps among them, returned to the ambush site the next day and buried the dismembered bodies of the three men of the advance party. They did not find Callaway's body, but his rifle was found a few days later, upright in the mud. Only when the flood waters receded more completely was Callaway's body discovered, caught in a bush. It was retrieved and interred nearby.[56]

First Lieutenant David Bailey subsequently took command and the company was transferred northeastward to the Cuivre River region. There, at Woods' Fort, William Becknell was discharged on June 20, 1815.[57]

He rode for St. Charles. Like most Rangers, Becknell had not been paid for much of his service:[58] He estimated the bankrupt Paymaster General owed him about $601. On August 18, 1815, Becknell appointed Richard Kerr to collect his back pay as Ensign in Callaway's Company in return for "divers goods, causes and consideration."[59] Thus endowed, Becknell reentered civilian life.

Little is known about William Becknell's activities during the ensuing months. He may have immediately entered the salt trade in central Missouri, a pursuit that apparently occupied much of his time for the remainder of the decade. Jane Trusler Becknell evidently had died, for, by

1817, Becknell was married to the former Mary Cribbs of Pennsylvania.[60] In that year a son was born in Howard County, the heart of "Boone's Lick Country." He was named William Alexander Becknell, Jr.[61]

The "Boone's Lick Country" of central Missouri received its name from a mercantile endeavor by Nathan and Daniel Morgan Boone. Nathan Boone and Mathias Van Bibber had discovered a brackish spring there in late 1804 while returning from a trapping expedition to the Kansas River during which they had been robbed by Osage Indians. Sometime during 1805, the Boone brothers ascended the Missouri, located the spring, and began "making salt." This saline spring, or "lick," was soon known as "Boone's Lick," and the name was gradually applied to an ever-increasing portion of central Missouri.[62]

By 1811, the year before Becknell's visit to the McKnight expedition at Boone's Lick, the region contained settlers who had cleared the wilderness in scattered locations along the Missouri River, and the land surrounding these settlements was beginning to gain notoriety. An English observer in one of John Jacob Astor's fur trading expeditions passed through the area and reported that:

> We encamped this night a little above the mouth of the Bonne Femme, a small river on the north side, where the tract of land, called Boond's [sic] Lick settlement, commences, supposed to be the best land in Western America for so great an area; it extends about 150 miles up the Missouri and is near 50 miles in breadth.[63]

William Becknell may have been in the region as early as 1811; an early settler reminisced that "ferrying was done here by Mr. Becknel [sic] in 1811. The crossing was made by having two canoes fastened together and a platform on top."[64]

In December, 1816, Becknell was at Cooper's Fort in the Boone's Lick Country. He and Julius and Ira Emmons contracted to take a keelboat and supplies owned by Joseph Robidoux III from Cooper's stockade to the garrison at Fort Osage upon arrival of the spring thaw. Robidoux in the interim would allow the three to use the keelboat to transport "salt and other goods" as far as St. Louis; they would then ascend the Missouri with goods obtained down river. Yet when the aspiring salt merchants piled their freight on the river bank in the midst of winter, Robidoux failed to supply the boat, and the salt was ruined.

Becknell and the Emmonses sued Robidoux for $2,000 damages in the April term of court in Howard County.[65] The case, continued in July, was finally settled — "Judgment for the defendant November Term 1817."[66]

Although Becknell was living at the Boone's Lick salt spring in November, 1817,[67] he had purchased lots 52 and 53 in the new village of Franklin the previous August,[68] and it was there that he served as a juror in a trespass case on November 11 and 12, 1817.[68]

Franklin, named in honor of Benjamin Franklin and the most flourishing township in the region, was begun in 1816 on the north bank of the Missouri River. It was the home of the *Missouri Intelligencer*, "probably the most important of the early newspapers outside of St. Louis."[70] Founded in 1817, the *Intelligencer* mirrored the development of the area, supplementing local news and advertisements with national and international news gleaned from newspapers of the larger eastern cities. In November, 1817, the *Intelligencer* reported:

> Immigration to this territory, and particularly to this country, during the present season, exceeds almost belief. Those who have arrived are principally from Kentucky and Tennessee. Immense numbers of wagons, carriages, carts, etc., with families have for some time past been arriving daily. During October it is stated that no less than 271 wagons and four-wheeled carriages and carts passed near St. Charles bound principally for Boone's Lick. It is calculated that the number of persons accompanying these wagons could not be less than 3,000. It is stated in the St. Louis Enquirer of the 10th inst. that about twenty wagons, etc., per week had passed through St. Charles for the past nine weeks with wealthy, respectable immigrants from various states whose numbers are supposed to amount to 12,000. The county of Howard, already respectable in numbers, will soon possess a vast population and no section of our country presents a fairer prospect to the immigrant.[71]

But Howard County, which encompassed present-day Callaway, Boone, Ray, Chariton, and Cooper counties, already possessed a remarkable citizenry. On the same 1817 tax roll with William Bicknell [*sic*] were Peter (Pierre) Chouteau, to be known as an entrepreneur of the fur trade a few years hence; Benjamin Cooper and Benjamin Cooper, Jr., of the pioneer Boone's Lick family and later Santa Fe Trail notables; and Harmon Gregg, whose eleven-year-old son, Josiah, would mature to write the classic account of the Santa Fe trade, *Commerce of the Prairies*, in 1844. Although they could not have foreseen it, Becknell and his neighbors in Boone's Lick Country were destined to make a monumental contribution to America's development.[72]

Old settlers and new created additional villages in the region. Booneville was established on the south bank of the Missouri opposite Franklin. Major Stephen H. Long, commander of a scientific expedition ascending the Missouri in 1819, described it as containing "eight houses, but having, in some respects, a more advantageous situation, and probably destined to rival if not surpass its neighbor."[73] Long's appraisal was prophetic. Five miles west of Booneville, across the La Mine River, stood the village of La Mine. Roughly ten miles to the north, on a promontory above the Missouri, stood Arrow Rock township. Across the Missouri, to the east, lay the Boone's Lick salt spring, and southeast of the spring sat thriving Franklin, perched on the bank of the great river.

The year 1818 was a busy one for William Becknell. On June 6, he was involved in a brawl with James Riggs at Franklin. Becknell soon found himself in Howard County Circuit Court facing charges that he "upon the plaintiff made an assault, and him then and there beat, bruised, wounded, and evil entreated, and other enormities to the plaintiff the said William then and there did, against the peace and dignity of the United States, and to the damage of the plaintiff five (?) hundred dollars . . . ." The cause of this donnybrook is uncertain, but Becknell seems to have given Riggs a sound thrashing. The defendant pleaded not guilty through his attorney, a Mr. Tompkins. Becknell was subsequently fined five dollars, no doubt to Riggs' further mortification.[74]

By autumn, William Becknell was a resident of La Mine township. The October 2, 1818 *Missouri Gazette and Public Advertiser* contained the following notice:

Taken Up

By Wm. Becknell as a stray, living in La Mine township, and county of Howard, a small sorrel mare, about fourteen hands high, eight or nine years old, both hind feet white, appraised to forty dollars, by Julius Emmonds [sic] and Starting Nuckolds appraisers, duly appointed and sworn for that purpose, this fifteenth day of July, 1818. Before me. Augustus Stores [sic], J. P.[75]

Becknell and the Emmonses were still associated. The partnership engaged in freighting, probably as a part-time endeavor, and is recorded as having lent $2.50 to an individual in Franklin in 1819.[76]

In late 1818, William Becknell purchased a ferry license from Sheriff Nicholas S. Burckhartt for a fee of $10.[77] The exact place of operation remains vague; however, all available accounts suggest the ferry operated in the Arrow Rock vicinity.[78] Hordes of settlers pouring into the region increased the demand for ferrying across the Missouri, and everyday commerce in the Boone's Lick Country required communication between the banks of the broad river. The ferrying business held obvious financial attractions for Becknell. Residually, participation in such a service offered the operator an opportunity to become well known, a valuable asset to anyone interested in running for public office. He evidently operated the ferry at intervals until at least December, 1826.[79]

Within a few months, Becknell was again working for James and Jesse Morrison, his pre-war employers, as manager of the Boone's Lick salt works. The Morrisons had furnished men and kettles to Nathan and Daniel Morgan Boone before 1810,[80] and by 1811 James Morrison had bought the "lick" from the Boones. Becknell may have worked there when he delivered the horse and gun to Robert McKnight in 1812. The wages then were fifteen dollars per month for either day or night shift. Even in the Boones' day, sixteen to twenty men labored over 120 kettles rendering 100 bushels of salt a day,[81] so Becknell's responsibilities were evidently considerable. Large kettles filled with brackish water offered little potential without fuel:

> The subscriber wishes to hire the cutting of from three to five hundred cords of wood, at the Boon's Lick salt works, for which he will give fifty cents per cord, and board the hands that cut it.
>
> William Becknell
> June 18 (1819)[82]

But this notice in the Franklin *Intelligencer* only hints at the realities of "salt making." The spring flowed from the earth in a hollow, forming a narrow stream bordered with white salt residue. The atmosphere was heavy with the odor of salt and sulphur, and the task of boiling many gallons of water on hot summer days must have taxed all involved. Danger was ever-present; James Morrison's sixteen-year-old son is said to have been scalded to death while working at the spring in 1833. Once obtained, the salt was freighted the short distance to the Missouri River and loaded onto boats for the twenty-eight-day voyage to St. Louis. The return journey, against the current, generally took forty days. The retail price of salt in Missouri in 1818 was $2.50 a bushel.[83]

Becknell may have become a partner of the Morrisons in late summer, 1819. On August 19, Becknell and his wife, Mary, sold one and three-quarter sections of land, obtained the previous April and May, to the Morrisons for $430.[84] This sum, or some other consideration, may have been used to "buy in" with the St. Charles entrepreneurs. A letter to the editor in the August 27 edition of the *Missouri Intelligencer*, signed by a correspondent using the sobriquet "Truth," stated that the original Boone's Lick salt springs were "now occupied by Messrs. Becknell & Morrisons."[85]

The dawn of a momentous new decade found William and Mary Becknell and their children, William A., John, and Cornealia, in a setting of bitter cold, with a thick blanket of snow.[86] An advertisement carried his name in the *Missouri Intelligencer* of January 7, 1820:

Strayed

From the subscriber, living at Boon's Lick, a small dark bay Mare, about 9 years old, branded thus II. and M. on the near shoulder. Any person who will deliver said mare shall receive five dollars.

Wm. Becknell[87]

The next day Becknell bought 160 acres in Howard County from Drury R. Prichard for $300.[88] This evidence of prosperity is offset by a $321 loan from Joseph Cooper on July 6, and a loan for $495.75 from Daniel Fall on July 21, 1820.[89] These loans signaled the beginning of hard times for William Becknell. During that same month he entered into Missouri politics.

By 1820, the Missouri Territory was in the frustrating process of gaining statehood. The nation-wide slavery issue caused months of delay in the acceptance of Missouri into the Union and much irritation among Missourians. On July 19, 1820, the Missouri convention adopted a state constitution and the convention president ordered a general election of state officials for August 28. Due to complications resolved by the Missouri Compromise, Missouri was not to be officially admitted to the Union until August 10, 1821. Nevertheless, arrangements for the August, 1820, election proceeded.

In a list of candidates for the House of Representatives from Howard County, published in the *Missouri Intelligencer* on July 29, 1820, was one "Capt. William Becknell."[90] He was among thirty-nine candidates in Howard County seeking a limited number of House seats; only forty-three seats were available for the entire state. Competing against him in the election were such notables as Colonel William Boon [sic] and General Duff Green.[91] Of a total of 12,235 votes cast in Howard County, William Becknell received 431, well behind the 565 for Boone and 636 for Green.[92]

Meanwhile, the nation was feeling the effects of the Panic of 1819, which struck especially hard in frontier areas like Missouri. The flood of settlers into the region, earlier greeted as a sign of great promise, brought land speculation and, in 1819, hard times. Farmers could not make payments on the land they had cleared and cultivated because their produce lost its value. They could not pay merchants for the goods they had used in the past or the necessities they would need in the future. Merchants were unable to sell goods they had on hand, for further extension of credit, under the circumstances, would be ruinous. The golden promise of the frontier had turned dark and barren.[93]

But William Becknell had a plan for delivering himself from debt. On April 21, 1821, he arranged with Thomas A. Smith to hire "three negro men . . . Aaron, Kain and Tom for the term of one year . . . at the rate of twelve dollars and fifty cents each, per month, . . . and one negro woman, Lucy, for one year at forty dollars a year." This action by "William Becknell & Co." was not a manifestation of debt-induced insanity; extra hands would be needed if Becknell's plans materialized.[94]

On May 29th, with the specter of financial ruin nipping at his heels, Becknell was taken into custody by Deputy Sheriff Benjamin Ray. Joseph Cooper wanted the $321 he had lent Becknell nearly eleven months earlier. James Jackson paid the $400 bond, and the case was scheduled for the July term of Howard County Circuit Court.[95]

Thus, through the generosity of a friend, William Becknell was spared the ignominy of facing his family and creditors through the bars of the Howard County jail. Instead, he was at liberty, preparing to inaugurate a momentous new era for himself, his neighbors, and his country.

Chapter II

On the Trail to Santa Fe

THE FRANKLIN *Missouri Intelligencer* of June 25, 1821, contained "An article for the government of a company of men destined to the westward for the purpose of trading Horses & Mules, and catching Wild Animals of every description, that we may think advantageous to the company." The lengthy notice by "Wm. Becknell," described in detail the responsibilities and relationships to be expected on the journey:

> Every man will fit himself for the trip with a horse, a good rifle, and as much ammunition as the company may think necessary for a tour or 3 month trip, & sufficient cloathing [*sic*] to keep him warm and comfortable. Every man will furnish his equal part of the fitting on for our trade, and receive an equal part of the product. If the company consist of 30 or more men, 10 dollars a man will answer to purchase the quantity of merchandise required to trade on.

> No man shall receive more than another for his services, unless he furnishes more, and is pointedly agreed on by the company before we start . . . . There will be no dividend until we return to the north side of the Missouri river, where all persons concerned shall have timely notice to attend and receive their share of the profits . . . . It is requisite that every 8 men shall have a pack horse, an ax, and a tent to secure them from the inclemency of bad weather . . . . It shall be my business to apply to the governor for permission to proceed as far as we wish to go. Signers to the amount of 70 will be received until the 4th of August, when every man wishing to go is requested to meet at Ezekiel Williams's, on the Missouri, about five miles above Franklin, where we will procure a pilot and appoint officers to the company.[1]

Becknell planned to take up to seventy men and several hundred dollars in merchandise on a westward journey of about three months' duration. They would go as far as they wished, anticipating a blessing from the governor, and trading for horses and mules and trapping wild game.

While reticent, William Becknell was far from reclusive. The desire for internal improvements financed by the federal government had long been a popular sentiment on the frontier. No wonder, then, that the cry for federal relief from the ravages of the Panic of 1819 was heard in places like Missouri. Becknell, his interest in politics still intact despite his earlier defeat at the polls, had definite ideas concerning the relief issue. His thoughts were enunciated at a gathering eloquently described by the *Missouri Gazette:*

> On Saturday, the 28th July, a splendid and elegant dinner was given at the Franklin Hotel by the citizens of Franklin and its vicinity to those members of the legislature who voted for the Relief Bill. A large and respectable concourse attended. Colonel Philip Tramell was chosen president and Capt. Jesse W. Garner vice president. The most perfect harmony and cordiality prevailed. After tho [*sic*] cloth was removed the following toasts were drunk: . . . By Captain William Becknell — The honourable Legislature; those who voted independently for the relief of the people of this state: may their zeal be duly appreciated by their constitutents.[2]

Four cheers followed Becknell's toast. There were eleven toasts in all and 126 cheers that evening, with a splendid time had by all.

While many in Boone's Lick Country looked east to Washington for financial salvation, William Becknell, even as he spoke to the assembly at Franklin, looked west. Before he could ride in that direction, however, he found himself deeper in dept.

On August 7, Becknell and the Morrison brothers visited Amos Ashcraft and borrowed $170 "bearing interest from the first day of February last. . . ." The note was signed "W. Becknell & Co."[3] Meanwhile, preparations for the trip continued.

Seventeen men assembled at Williams' farm at the appointed time to organize the expedition. The *Intelligencer* of August 14, 1821, carried a report from Becknell:

> W. Becknell was chosen by a unanimous vote as Captain to the company. On the 18th inst. we are all to meet at Mr. Shaw's in

Franklin, where two Lieutenants will be elected. We have concluded that thirty men will constitute a company sufficiently strong to proceed as far as we wish to go. All those who signed their names to the first article, and did not appear on the 4th of this month, are excluded from going in this company, and excused from paying any fine. On the first day of September, the company will cross the Missouri at Arrow Rock. Any persons who wish to go will do well to meet at the place appointed on the 18th. No signers will be received after that day.

W. Becknell[4]

Again Becknell's reference to his planned destination was in vague words — "as far as we wish to go." More significant, however, is the fact that Ezekiel Williams' cabin was chosen for the first meeting.

William Becknell had known Ezekiel Williams since at least April, 1817, when Williams served as a juryman in the suit brought against Joseph Robidoux by Becknell.[5] Williams was also perhaps the only one of Becknell's neighbors with considerable experience on the Great Plains and beyond. In 1811, as an employee of the St. Louis Missouri Fur Company, owned in part by Manuel Lisa, Williams had participated in Jean Baptiste Champlain's ill-fated expedition to the upper Arkansas river. He descended the Arkansas alone in March, 1813, the only member of the party to avoid death on the plains or imprisonment in Santa Fe.[6] In May, 1814, after spending more than a year in Missouri, he returned to the Arkansas to recover furs he had cached there, accompanied by partners Braxton Cooper and Morris May as well as eighteen Frenchmen commanded by Joseph Philibert. Williams, Cooper, and May salvaged part of the cache and retreated to Missouri while Philibert's Frenchmen ventured to the upper Arkansas where they were subsequently apprehended by the Spanish. The party was released in the spring of 1815.[7]

Ezekiel Williams, therefore, had considerable experience on the plains, was familiar with much of the country, and knew a number of men who had ventured too close to New Mexico and had been allowed, as prisoners, a glimpse of the forbidden province. He had several interesting stories to tell the seventeen eager and curious Missourians who met at his home on that August day in 1821.

Captain Becknell and his associates must have wondered about the nature of the land they would enter. Beyond the last outposts of civilization in Missouri, the woodlands scattered into clusters and hardwood eventually vanished altogether. There, cottonwood furnished the only semblance of timber to be found, and then usually only in stream beds. Buffalo manure could be used to fuel a fire, since cottonwood was not suitable for cooking. The few broad but comparatively shallow rivers and their tributaries contrasted sharply with the more numerous waterways of the East. The Arkansas, with its sand banks and quicksand hazards, had water too alkaline to drink at some points. The rivers were often separated by vast expanses of flat, seemingly barren wilderness covered with short grasses.[8] Despite this apparent desolation, large numbers of bison, antelope, and many other kinds of animals managed to thrive, providing the mainstay of life for various Indian tribes. Nomadic tribes ranged widely across the land, displaying different degrees of cooperation with whites. These independent horsemen bartered furs for manufactured goods with traders bold enough to approach them, but they also engaged in theft and murder on occasion. Farther west lay the Rocky Mountains, where rivers such as the Platte and Arkansas were born. Spanish patrols from New Mexico guarded the upper Arkansas, for Spain was intent upon defending and regulating what was hers.

Rivalry between Spain and France had caused the Spanish government to be especially vigilant along its North American border. French traders from Illinois visited Santa Fe as early as 1739, and others followed at intervals. There was potential danger in allowing these foreigners to bring merchandise into the province, fraternize with the inhabitants, and possibly arm neighboring Indians. Spanish officials, therefore, practiced confiscation and imprisonment in an effort to discourage interlopers.[9]

Spain's rule over Louisiana, from 1763 to 1803, buffered New Mexico and other provinces against foreign encroachment. All this changed in 1803 when the United States bought the vast Louisiana Territory. Spanish officials in the northern provinces sought to keep thousands of miles of border wilderness from being invaded and exploited by bands of American trappers, traders, and filibusters. The failure of the United States and Spain to agree upon a definite boundary between their holdings until the Adams-Onín Treaty of 1819 exacerbated the problem. In the meantime, as one historian put it, "both governments claimed more than they expected to get."[10]

This border dispute partially explains the hostile attitude of the governors of New Mexico toward Americans. The Spanish province of Texas in particular saw several invasions of armed filibusters from the United States. In 1812, for example, the Gutiérrez-Magee expedition succeeded in capturing the three main Texas settlements of Nacogdoches, Goliad, and San Antonio. Mexican revolutionaries who comprised a part of the expedition took advantage of the conquest to declare Texas "a part of the Mexican Republic" after butchering the vanquished Spanish Governor Manuel María de Salcedo. Some Anglo-Americans disagreed strongly with both of these developments and returned to the United States. "The Republican Army of North," as the expedition called itself, defeated a Spanish Army at Alazan Creek in June, 1813, but was finally beaten back in August of that year by a 2,000-man army under the Spanish General Joaquín de Arredondo. A brutal bloodbath followed in which hundreds of filibusters and their supporters were executed without trial.[11]

Thus, it is not surprising that Spanish officials anywhere near United States territory were vigilant. Although New Mexico was spared invasion on the scale seen in Texas, the arrival of any armed group, no matter how small or peaceful their business, might portend trouble. Far-ranging bands of trappers and traders from the United States could not be allowed to develop close ties with Indians and Spanish subjects if security were to be maintained. These uninvited visitors were deprived of their goods, taken to Santa Fe for questioning, and usually sent to prison deep in Mexico. Only a few managed to return to the United States, empty-handed but more knowledgeable about New Mexico.

At the same time that they held American traders at arm's length, New Mexicans languished under a monopoly of trade imposed on them by government restrictions. The Chihuahua trail was the only authorized trade route between New Mexico and the interior, but it left the province "in constant debt and short of manufactured goods." The inhabitants would gladly have welcomed cheaper and more plentiful trade goods from the United States if only their government would allow it, but permission to engage in trade with *extranjeros* was forbidden until the last day of Spanish rule in New Mexico in September, 1821.[12]

As Mexico struggled for independence in 1821, William Becknell and his associates were poised on the Missouri, ready to begin their journey west. In November, 1821, they would arrive in Santa Fe. Was this development accidental or planned? Becknell would not likely have risked spending years in a Spanish dungeon on a blind gamble. He knew that the McKnight party had ventured west in 1812 under the assumption that Father Miguel Hidalgo's revolutionaries had won control of the Mexican government and that trade with foreigners would be allowed in New Mexico. Robert McKnight and his men were captured and imprisoned for eight years. Becknell was also aware that a new revolt had begun in Mexico. General Agustín de Iturbide had proclaimed the Plan of Iguala on February 24, 1821, asserting, but not securing, Mexican independence five months before Becknell placed his initial call for men in the Franklin newspaper. This and other news from Mexico may have convinced Becknell that his chances of suffering McKnight's fate were greatly reduced. Furthermore, he could have known something of the governor of New Mexico, Facundo Melgares, "described by Zebulon Pike as a man with 'a high sense of honor,' . . . known to be friendly toward Americans, and in the crunch the Governor's attitude was apt to be more important than restrictive laws."[13]

Becknell's arrival in New Mexico seems to have been no accident; he prepared as thoroughly as possible with that end in mind. Becknell counselled with Ezekiel Williams, conceivably about the nature of the proposed route and the likelihood of contacting receptive New Mexican patrols on the far side of the Great Plains. Becknell probably refrained from publicizing his destination for fear of competition, perhaps not wanting to forewarn Spanish diplomats in the United States where he was bound.[14] As far as he knew, the revolution in Mexico had not been crushed; therefore, the time was right to begin, especially since further delay could only exacerbate his troubles in Missouri.

On August 21, 1821, Becknell incongruously purchased a half section of land in the western part of Howard County.[15] Perhaps the expectation of a highly successful venture west engendered this action, but it could only serve to enrage his creditors.

William Becknell's financial problems culminated in at least five law suits in Howard County Circuit Court in late 1821 and the first months of 1822, all while he was on his westward journey. Indeed, creditors descended upon his property before his absence was a week old. On September 7, 1821, Sheriff Burckhardt executed a writ of attachment against Becknell, seizing "one hundred salt kettles, one Negro Girl Slave named Sally, twenty Barrels of Salt, the Northwest quarter of Section Number Six & the South west quarter of the same Section in Township number forty nine of Range No. Seventeen."[16]

On September 17, Henry V. Bingham, administrator of the estate of the late Daniel Fall, filed suit on behalf of the estate to force Becknell's payment of the $495.75 in loans Fall had granted in July, 1820.[17] The court decided during the January term, 1822, "that unless he [Becknell] shall appear by himself or attorney, and file special bail to the action aforesaid of said plaintiff, on or before the third day of the next term of court, a judgement will be entered up against him, and his estate sold to satisfy the same."[18]

Meanwhile, Joseph Cooper's suit had been decided in the November term of court. Judge David Todd found that "the said William Becknell did not well and truly pay to the said Joseph Cooper the said sum of money in the declaration mentioned in manner and form as the said William Becknell in his said plea hath alledged . . ." and that Becknell was to pay Cooper $291.27 plus court costs and fees incurred in recovering the debt.[19]

Even Becknell's doctor, Hardage Lane, came forward with a law suit during the November term, seeking $120 for professional services and eighty dollars in damages from his absent patient. The case was to be heard during the March court term. Then, on November 8, Deputy Sheriff Ray executed a writ of attachment in the Lane case by taking possession of one of Becknell's slaves, a man named Mark.[20]

The November term of Judge Todd's court also saw a suit brought against "William Becknell and others" by Thomas Thewt. The "others" were Jesse and James Morrison, Becknell's partners at the Boone's Lick salt works. The court decided "that the said defendants did undertake and promise in manner and form as the said plaintiff has above thereof in his declaration complained against them, and assess the damages of the said plaintiff by him sustained . . . to the sum of one hundred and eight dollars and forty cents. Therefore it is considered that the said William Becknell, Jesse Morrison, & James Morrison pay his damages aforesaid. . . ."[21]

William Becknell and the Morrison brothers were also sued by Amos Ashcraft, who had loaned "W. Becknell & Co." $170 the previous August. The plaintiff sought to confront his debtors in the January term of court, but apparently none of the defendants could be found. At this juncture, Judge Todd, "On motion of the plaintiff by his attorney ordered that an alias summons be issued herin & also a Counterpart to the County of St. Charles." Later in the January term an "Alias writ" was issued in both Howard and St. Charles counties.[22] Becknell had vanished onto the plains more than four months earlier; his co-defendants were presumed to be in seclusion in Howard County or perhaps St. Charles County.

William Becknell's journey west was clearly an act of desperation. He was hundreds of dollars in debt and his salt business was in ruins. All his adult life had been spent in Missouri, fighting for the land and helping to develop it. Above all, his family must have been his prime concern. Everything he cherished was at stake.

If William Becknell's problems prompted his venture onto the plains, the plight of Mary Becknell might well be imagined. Her husband gone, perhaps dead, it was her ordeal to witness the deluge of court actions against him and to uphold the family honor until, or if, her husband should return.

William Becknell and his companions[23] began their journey west on schedule, September 1, 1821. The only extant firsthand account of their adventure appeared nearly two years later, on April 22, 1823, in the *Franklin Intelligencer and Boone's Lick Advertiser.* Entitled "Journal of two Expeditions from Boon's Lick to Santa Fe," the article was introduced as "the journal of Capt. William Becknell."[24] The polished style in which it was written indicates that William Becknell did not write it, for although he could write, his grammar and spelling were poor. Furthermore, the introduction expressed the hope that the journal would "impress distant readers with an idea of the boldness and activity of their western brethren." The possibility that the journal was a fictitious creation of the publisher of the *Intelligencer*, designed to provide a glamorized account of the journey to a receptive public, has been speculated upon by scholars interested in the subject. Some question its value as a valid source.[25]

While it is impossible to verify the source of the journal, some consideration of the circumstances under which it was written may shed light on the matter. The journal appeared in the *Intelligencer* more than a year after Becknell's return from New Mexico. Although Becknell left members of his expedition in New Mexico, some may have returned home in the interim. The opportunity for Becknell and his associates to discuss their adventure with neighbors in Boone's Lick Country could have occurred on any one of countless occasions. The publisher of the *Intelligencer* could scarcely afford to print a blatantly fictionalized version of Becknell's journey with members of the party walking the streets of Franklin ready to correct any inaccuracies. Furthermore, we may question if Captain William Becknell would subject himself and his family to the ridicule resulting from such a shady undertaking.

The journal is, after all, not that sensational. It is plausible that Becknell presented a rough manuscript or oral account to the publisher of the *Intelligencer*, or some other more literate person, and that the intermediary transformed Becknell's rustic version of the journey into a more readable style.[26] The introduction described the journal as "an unvarnished revelation of circumstances," and warned that it "perhaps may not present the reader with that entertainment and gratification of his curiosity which his fancy may anticipate." This appraisal of the "journal of Capt. William Becknell" may, under the circumstances, be fairly valid.

Another much-cited source concerning Becknell's first journey to New Mexico appeared in 1844, with the publication of Missourian Josiah Gregg's *Commerce of the Prairies*. Gregg stated that Becknell ventured West "with the original purpose of trading with the Iatan or Comanche Indians," and that his arrival in Santa Fe resulted from "having fallen in accidentally with a party of Mexican rangers."[27] Generations of scholars have accepted Gregg's account as fact, but close examination of Becknell's journal reveals a different interpretation.[28] The discrepancies between these two sources become apparent as William Becknell's story unfolds.

According to Becknell's account, his party traveled six miles on September 1, after crossing the Missouri at Arrow Rock. The weather was initially conducive to travel but deteriortated to the point that it caused "some inconvenience" due to rain and cold. Arriving at Fort Osage, Missouri, some eleven miles east of present day Kansas City, members of the expedition "wrote letters, purchased some medicines, and arranged such affairs as we thought necessary previous to leaving the confines of civilization." Becknell apparently wrote a letter to his wife which reached Franklin sometime around September 30, 1821.[29]

The government factor at Fort Osage was George C. Sibley, who had special knowledge of Santa Fe to share with Becknell. In a letter to his brother speculating upon possible war with England and Spain in 1808, he had stated that "this will be a rallying post from whence to attack Santa Fee [*sic*] . . . ."[30] Furthermore, Sibley had boarded in the home of Dr. John H. Robinson, a member of Zebulon Pike's expedition of 1806. Not only had Robinson seen Santa Fe, but he had also mapped Pike's route during the journey. Later, as deputy Indian Agent, Robinson was a visitor at Fort Osage, and various aspects of the Mexican north were doubtless topics of conversation between Sibley and Robinson. Becknell may have drawn upon Sibley's knowledge of what lay "to the westward," perhaps collating it with Ezekiel Williams' observations. Becknell used Sibley's Fort Osage as the jumping off point for this and subsequent journeys across the plains, and the two men would later participate in a government-backed marking and grading project of the Santa Fe Trail. George Sibley later described the Becknell he knew in 1821 as:

> . . . a man of good character, great personal bravery, & by nature & habit hardy and enterprising. He certainly had no knowledge of merchantile concerns, & is tho' very shrewd and intelligent, very deficient in education.[31]

Four days after leaving Fort Osage, Becknell became ill after a vigorous and unsuccessful elk hunt. Others in the party were taken sick and progress was slowed. They reached the Osage River on September 20 and crossed it although they were "all sick and much discouraged." Heavy rain forced them to make camp. A large herd of buffalo was sighted the next day and one was killed, while several "goats" — presumably antelope — eluded them. At length, Becknell's party arrived at a tributary of the Arkansas River after crossing a flint-strewn prairie. The Missourians saw vast herds of buffalo as they plodded along and finally reached the white sand banks of the Arkansas on September 24. They crossed a branch of the river, remaining on the north side.

At this juncture, Becknell observed "it is a circumstance of surprise to us that we have seen no Indians, or fresh signs of them, although we have traversed their most frequented hunting grounds; but considering their furtive habits and predatory dispostion, the absence of their company during our journey, will not be a matter of regret."

This statement may be taken at face value as a noteworthy indication that Becknell did not intend to trade with Indians and planned to do business at the only other destination possible, New Mexico. The possibility exists, however, that Becknell, or his collaborator, used hindsight in writing this passage. Becknell had twice visited New Mexico by the time that the journal appeared, and it must have been evident that a distribution of the party's trade goods among the Indians would have precluded that history-making arrival in Santa Fe. Becknell's thoughts that autumn day on the banks of the Arkansas may never be known unless this part of the journal is credible.

Becknell's company crossed the Arkansas at a shallow ford and camped on the south bank. They entered a prairie dog village "about noon" the next day, and the frisky inhabitants clearly excited Becknell's curiosity. He killed and sampled the flesh of one of the rodents and pronounced it "strong and unpalatable." The party also encountered a species of rabbit with which they were unfamiliar — the jackrabbit. The Missourians were clearly in a strange land filled with exotic animals, but they were apparently not intimidated by it at all.

On the evening of September 28, Becknell and his associates made camp near some white sand hills they had observed during the day's travel. Buffalo chips were used to fuel the camp fires since vegetation was scarce. Torrential rains fell incessantly during the night, and the tents which the men carried provided "very comfortable" shelter. A buffalo was killed for breakfast early the next morning and by early afternoon the party approached "the celebrated salt plain of the Arkansas," a mile-wide stretch of salty sand, covered at the time by three inches of water, perhaps, as Becknell speculated, "owing to the late heavy rains." Emerging from the boggy region, Becknell observed that "the country here appears alive with buffalo and other animals. About this time we saw five wild horses, being the first we had seen." The company also witnessed an attack made by wolves on a hapless buffalo. According to Becknell, "a company of from ten to twenty divide into two parties, one of which separates a buffaloe [*sic*] from his herd, and pursues him, while the others head him. I counted twenty-one wolves one morning in a chase of this kind."

On October 15, the company arrived at a lake "which gave every appearance of being strongly impregnated with saltpetre" and the weary, still ailing Missourians camped there for three days. Their horses had become weak due to the grinding pace of the journey and the "unfitness of their food." Members of the group fashioned moccasins and hunted game while the horses regained strength.

The 21st of October found Becknell's company at a fork in the Arkansas. It was decided to take "the course of the left hand one." This placed them on a more southerly course, but it is uncertain whether the river they now followed was the Purgatoire, which they would have seen first, or the Timpas, some twenty-five miles to the west.[32] The terrain became more forbidding: "The cliffs become immensely high, and the aspect of the country is rugged, wild and dreary."

A distant gunshot rang out late on October 23, which Becknell and his men assumed was "the first indication of our being in the neighborhood of Indians." Whatever excitement the incident caused among the Missourians, nothing came of it, and the weary band plodded on.

Becknell and his men had now been on the trail almost two months. They had apparently seen no other human beings since leaving western Missouri. Becknell recorded that "as yet we have encountered no difficulty for water, but have been destitute of bread or even salt for several weeks." Their diet relied heavily on available game, and on October 26, one of a large herd of mountain sheep was killed and eaten. The land of the mountain sheep proved to be less easily traversed than the plains.

At one point during the last week of October, the travelers found their progress blocked by an imposing palisade of cliffs and spent two days clearing a path up the boulder-strewn barrier.[33] Despite their strenuous efforts, one of their horses lost its footing and tumbled down the face of the cliff to its death. The weary band then rode two days across an open plain before arriving at the Canadian River, where they again faced cliffs that were negotiated "with considerable difficulty."

On November 1, traveling a south-southwesterly course, the long-suffering Missourians were lashed by a blustery wind from the northwest accompanied by light snow. Becknell observed:

> Having been now travelling about fifty days, our diet being altogether different from what we had been accustomed to; and unexpected hardships and obstacles occuring almost daily, our company is much discouraged; but the prospect of a near termination of our journey excites hope and redoubled exertion, although our horses are so reduced that we only travel from eight to fifteen miles per day. We found game scarce near the mountains, and one night encamped without wood or water.

Becknell's party was in northeastern New Mexico, traveling a course roughly parallel to the Rio Grande River, separated from the New Mexican settlements along the river by the Sangre de Cristo Mountains. Becknell's journal seems to indicate that his party had some idea of their proximity to the "termination" they sought. Furthermore, it tends to discredit the theory that the party left Missouri with the intention of trading with Indians.[34] Had this been their goal, they had displayed monumental ineptitude by traversing 800 miles of Indian country without completing one business transaction or even seeing an Indian. Something was apparently driving them onward, for they had endured so much and come so far without turning back.

During the first week in November, Becknell's party entered more level terrain and saw scores of wild horses. Then "on Monday the 12th we struck a trail, and found several other indications which induced us to believe that the inhabitants had here herded their cattle and sheep." The group camped among the cottonwood and pine trees that evening, conceivably much excited about their discovery. They did not have to wonder long about its significance for

> On Tuesday morning the 13th, we had the satisfaction of meeting a party of Spanish troops. Although the difference of our language would not admit of conversation, yet the circumstances attending their reception of us, fully convinced us of their hospitable disposition and friendly feelings. Being likewise in a strange country, and subject to their dispostion,

our wishes lent their aid to increase our confidence in their manifestations of kindness.

Becknell and his associates, escorted by the army patrol, traveled the remainder of the day and camped that evening. The "Spaniards" led them into the village of San Miguel del Bado at about one o'clock the next day where the "inhabitants gave us grateful evidence of civility and welcome."

Whatever lingering apprehensions Becknell and his men may have felt were probably dispelled somewhat when they encountered a "Frenchman" in the village. Becknell recounts that "fortunately I here met with a Frenchman, whose language I imperfectly understand, and hired him to proceed with us to Santa Fe, in the capacity of an interpreter." Perhaps the "Frenchman" conveyed to Becknell that New Mexican officials had embraced the cause of Mexican independence two months earlier and that restrictions on trade with outsiders had been lifted.[35] Becknell and company at least knew they were not the only foreigners in the province.

The Missourians and their interpreter were escorted out of San Miguel the next morning. The entourage passed the village of "St. Baw" during the day and, after camping for the night, traversed "a mountainous country" before arriving at Santa Fe, Friday, November 16, 1821. Their reception was one of "apparent pleasure and joy."

Santa Fe, when Becknell first saw it, was "about two miles long and one mile wide, and compactly settled." It was the seat of the provincial government, administered by Governor Facundo Melgares. It also possessed a jail, into which Becknell and his men might have been thrown had they arrived a few months earlier. Other lodgings were found for the strangers, however, and the next day Becknell "accepted an invitation to visit the Governor."

Becknell's audience with Melgares went well. He found Don Facundo "well informed and gentlemanly in manners; his demeanor was courteous and friendly." Furthermore,

> He asked many questions respecting my country, its people, their manner of living, & c.; expressed a desire that the Americans would keep up an intercourse with that country, and said that if any of them wished to emigrate, it would give him pleasure to afford them every facility.

Questions arise as to the veracity of Becknell's account of the meeting. Did Melgares have the authority to open the province to trade with the United States and settlement by immigrants from the United States?

Would he risk his position and possibly his life to welcome Becknell in such a manner?[36] Historian Marc Simmons has described two documents that may have caused Governor Melgares to react as Becknell says he did.

Simmons found two circulars in the Mexican Archives of New Mexico in Santa Fe which were printed and "issued from Mexico City about mid-1821 to all provincial officers." Simmons argues that one of these documents

> contains a specific clause on the subject of trade, which in itself would have been sufficient to permit Governor Melgares to welcome William Becknell and other Americans.

This circular futher declared that ". . . With respect to foreign nations, we shall maintain harmony with all, commercial relations, and whatever else may be appropriate." Indeed, William Wolfskill, who accompanied Becknell on his second journey to New Mexico, later recalled that "Becknell had some kind of contract to supply the Mexican government with gunpowder, a product extremely scarce."[37]

Becknell stayed in New Mexico almost a month, ample time to trade with the inhabitants and observe their way of life. Reflecting the prejudices of his time and place, Becknell described his hosts as "generally swarthy," and living "in a state of extreme indolence and ignorance." Reflecting upon meeting the military patrol that escorted his party to Santa Fe, Becknell noted that "the discipline of the officers was strict, and the subjection of the men appeared almost servile." Indeed, the civilians were not much different: "like the French, they live in villages; the rich keeping the poor in dependence and subjection. Laborers are hired for about three dollars per month: their general employment is that of herdsmen . . ." Becknell evidently felt superior to the New Mexican peons: they accepted a social status and mode of living he clearly found distasteful.[38]

Becknell, the erstwhile farmer, found New Mexican agricultural methods of interest:

> Corn, rice and wheat are their principal production; they have very few garden vegetables except the onion, which grows large and abundantly; the seeds are planted nearly a foot apart, and produce onions from four to six inches in diameter. Their atmosphere is remarkably dry, and rain is uncommon except in the months of July and August. To remedy this inconvenience, they substitute, with tolerable advantage, the numerous streams which descend from the mountains, by

daming them up, and conveying the water over their farms in ditches. Their domestic animals consist chiefly of sheep, goats, mules and asses. None but the wealthy have horses and hogs.

As in Missouri, the chief predators in this pastoral province were Indians, "Navohoes [sic] who sometimes murder the guards and drive away their mules and sheep."

Even the dwellings and furniture of this exotic land were described by Becknell in his journal. He had learned much during his stay in New Mexico, but the most important information had been revealed in the governor's office at Santa Fe.

The Missourians must have returned to San Miguel sometime during the next three weeks, for it was there that Becknell left all but one of his men when he began his return trip to Missouri. Why these traders elected to stay behind is not stated in the journal; however, their decision was conceivably made on the basis of reports that other Americans had arrived in the province. Indeed, a party of trappers and traders led by John McKnight and Thomas James entered Santa Fe on December 1, 1821: the monopoly on American trade goods in New Mexico enjoyed by Becknell's party had lasted a brief two weeks.[39] Perhaps Becknell's men remained in New Mexico to consolidate or expand mercantile connections while their leader went to Missouri for more merchandise. They may also have hoped to engage in trapping.

Though the advent of competition may have hastened, it did not occasion Becknell's departure for Missouri. He had estimated in his first advertisement in the Franklin *Missouri Intelligencer* that an investment of ten dollars per man would suffice to purchase enough trade goods if there were thirty members in the company. Assuming that the value of their merchandise approximated three hundred dollars, and considering that the goods were transported by pack animal and therefore of limited quantity, one month in the receptive New Mexican market should have been enough time to exhaust or greatly diminish the party's stock.

Becknell left San Miguel on December 13, accompanied by a "Mr. M'Laughlin" who was one of his men, and "two other men who had arrived there a few days before, by a different route." Whether these "two other men" were former members of the McKnight-James party is a matter of conjecture, for Becknell did not mention the arrival of that company or any other in his journal.

Becknell had decided to use wagons on his return trip from Missouri, and this would preclude crossing Raton Pass. Therefore, he experimented with an alternate route and "on the 17th day of our journey, we arrived at the Arkansas, & thence shaped our course over the high land which separates the waters of that and the Caw rivers."

After buying corn from friendly Caw, or Kansas, Indians, the journey resumed and "in forty-eight days from the time of our departure we reached home, much to our satisfaction. We did not experience half the hardships anticipated, on our return." Snow, rain, gusty winds and a scarcity of firewood were their chief obstacles. More important is the fact that Becknell had shortened the route between Missouri and New Mexico from two-and-a-half months to forty-eight days.

The circumstances of Becknell's arrival in Franklin on January 30, 1822, are not clear. He probably rode into the village in a state of breathless anticipation; he had not seen his family for five months. The only extant account of the homecoming is a bit of oral history related years later by H. H. Harris, whose father evidently was a neighbor of Becknell's in Franklin:[40]

> My father saw them unload when they returned, and when their rawhide packages of silver dollars were dumped on the sidewalk one of the men cut the thongs and the money spilled out and clinking on the stone pavement rolled into the gutter. Everyone was excited and the next spring another expedition was sent out.[41]

The validity of this account may be questioned. Still the thought of William Becknell embracing his wife and children to the sound of cascading wealth and gasps of awe-struck neighbors is too delicious to ignore. Developments in Howard County Court provide more convincing evidence of Becknell's success.

Judge David Todd's records for the May term of Howard County Circuit Court reveal that at least two creditors decided not to continue their suits against Becknell. Details of both events were recorded consecutively on the same page and evidently took place the same day or on two successive days. Dr. Hardage Lane's law suit, initiated the previous November, was dealt with first:

> Now at this day comes the plaintiff aforesaid by his attorney aforesaid and says he will not further prosecute his action aforesaid against the said defendant, but permits the same to discontinue for want of prosecution. Therefore it is considered by the court that the said plaintiff take nothing by his writ

aforesaid and that the said defendant go thereof without day.
and recover against the said plaintiff his costs and charges
herein expended.

The next entry concerned the suit brought by Henry V. Bingham to
recover the $495.75 allegedly owed him by Becknell: Becknell's
homestead was at stake. The wording of the entry was exactly the same as
that used in discontinuing the Lane suit. Thus, William Becknell was
relieved of a substantial portion of his indebtedness.[42]

The most obvious explanation for this turn of events is that Becknell returned from New Mexico with enough valuables to repay at least part of
his debts. Perhaps he placated the plaintiffs with an arrangement concerning his planned return to New Mexico. Becknell's legal problems,
however, did not vanish entirely as a result of his first visit to New Mexico,
although it is certain that his western venture alleviated his financial
problems to some degree.

Chapter III

From Trail to Roadway

BECKNELL SPENT the next three-and-a-half months organizing his second expedition to Santa Fe. In addition to his own funds, he may have purchased trade goods with money belonging to the men left behind in New Mexico. Various residents of Boone's Lick country apparently invested in the venture as well, for one H. H. Harris recalled "one young lady, Miss Fanny Marshall, who put $60 in the expedition and her brother brought back $900 as her share."[1]

The profits realized by Becknell's second trip would be offset by hardships experienced on the trail. Becknell's journal indicates, however, that the expedition began auspiciously, much like the first:

> Having made arrangements to return, on the 22nd day of May, 1822, I crossed the Arrow Rock ferry, and on the third day our company, consisting of 21 men, with *three wagons*, concentrated. No obstacle obstructed our progress until we arrived at the Arkansas, which river we crossed with some difficulty, and encamped on the south side.

Italics were used by the publisher of the *Intelligencer* for good reason; Becknell's second journal marked the first use of wagons on the Santa Fe Trail. The importance of this development was thus clearly recognized by those concerned as early as the next spring.

The efforts made by Becknell the previous December to make his next journey to New Mexico less hazardous were somewhat negated one mid-June night when

> About midnight our horses were frightened by buffaloes, and all strayed — 28 were missing. Eight of us, after appointing a place of rendezvous, went in pursuit of them in different directions, and found eighteen. Two of this company discovered some indians, and being suspicious of their intentions, thought to avoid them by returning to camp; but they were overtaken,

stripped, barbarously whipped, and robbed of their horses, guns and clothes. They came in about midnight, and the circumstances occasioned considerable alarm. We had a strong desire to punish the rascally Osages, who commit outrages on those very citizens from whom they receive regular annuities. One other man was taken by the same party to their camp, and probably would have shared like treatment, had not the presence of Mr. Choteau restrained their savage dispositions. He sent word to me that he had recovered the horses and guns which had been taken from our men, and requested me to come on the next morning and receive them. On our arrival at his camp we found it evacuated, but a short note written on bark instructed me to follow him up the Autawge river. This we declined, thinking that his percipitate retreat indicated some strategem or treachery.

That Becknell chose not to be distracted further by this event is not surprising; he was a man in a hurry. Competition was already on the trail. Colonel Benjamin Cooper's fifteen-man expedition had left Missouri several days ahead of Becknell. The Glenn-Fowler party, returning to Missouri from New Mexico that summer, encountered the Cooper expedition at the Big Bend of the Arkansas on July 12. Another party, headed by John Heath, followed Becknell's wagon tracks.[2]

Becknell's journal states that "Mr. Heath's company on the same route joined us here." Becknell's men were still smarting from their treatment at the hands of the Indians.

The hiliarity [sic] and sociability of the gentlemen often contributed to disperse the gloomy images which very naturally presented themselves on a journey of such adventure and uncertainty. After six days of incessant fatigue in endeavoring to recover all our horses, we once more left our camp, and after traveling eight days up the Arkansas, struck a southwest course for the Spanish country.

This "southwest course" was a significant departure from Becknell's first route. It eliminated dangerous Raton Pass, but necessitated the crossing of the arid region between the Arkansas and Cimarron rivers. This more level route thereafter became an established section of the Santa Fe Trail and, together with Becknell's use of wagons, wins him the title of "Father of the Santa Fe Trail."[3]

Becknell's journal says little about this history-making part of the passage except that "our greatest difficulty was in the vicinity of Rock river, where we were under the necessity of taking our waggons [sic] up some high and rocky cliffs by hand." Rock river, a tributary of the Canadian River, was well past the dry expanse between the Arkansas and the Cimarron.

Josiah Gregg, in his renowned *Commerce of the Prairies*, published in 1844, relates a drastically different account of Becknell's trek from the Arkansas to the Cimarron:

> With no other guide but the starry heavens, and, it may be, a pocket-compass, the party embarked upon the arid plains which extended far and wide before them to the Cimarron River. The adventurous band pursued their forward course without being able to procure any water, except from the scanty supply they carried in their canteens. As this source of relief was completely exhausted after two days' march, the sufferings of both men and beasts had driven them almost to distraction. The forlorn band were at last reduced to the cruel necessity of killing their dogs, and cutting off the ears of their mules, in the vain hope of assuaging their burning thirst with the hot blood.

The dramatic measures described by Gregg only increased their thirst. Members of the group scoured the countryside in a frenzied attempt to find water. Tortured by mirages, the desperate travelers conceivably huddled in the shade provided by their three motionless wagons and discussed their options. It was decided that they would follow their tracks back to the Arkansas, "not suspecting (as was the case) that they had already arrived near the banks of the Cimarron. . . ." Perhaps some feeble effort toward implementing this plan took place, but as Gregg told it, they

> would undoubtedly have perished in those arid regions, had not a buffalo, fresh from the river's side, and with a stomach distended with water, been discovered by some of the party, just as the last rays of hope were receding from their vision. The hapless intruder was immediately dispatched, and an invigorating draught procured from its stomach . . . . they succeeded in reaching Taos (sixty or seventy miles north of Santa Fe) without further difficulty.[4]

Gregg's well-known account of the Becknell party's tribulations contrasts sharply with Becknell's journal. Becknell does not mention this harrowing event nor does he recount a retreat to the Arkansas or an arrival in Taos. The journal states that "we arrived again at St. Michael [San Miguel] in 22 days from the Arkansas." Taos and San Miguel were approximately eighty miles apart, separated by the Sangre de Cristo Mountains, and were, in fact, on two distinctly different routes to Santa Fe. Furthermore, Becknell had spent seventeen days traveling to the Arkansas from San Miguel on his way back to Missouri the previous winter, while it took twenty-two days to cover nearly the same ground on his return trip to San Miguel that next summer. The five-day difference may be explained by the reduced rate of travel inherent in the use of wagons; a circuitous route by way of Taos and Santa Fe is clearly implausible.

Still, the possibility that Becknell's company suffered an incident such as that described in *Commerce of the Prairies* cannot be totally discounted, for Gregg relates that "I have since heard one of the parties to that expedition declare, that nothing ever passed his lips which gave him such exquisite delight as his first draught of that filthy beverage [from the buffalo's stomach]."[5] The possibility exists that William Becknell was the source of this information, for Gregg visited the area where Becknell lived in August, 1841, three years before *Commerce of the Prairies* was published.[6] Furthermore, Becknell mentioned his avoidance of "the so much dreaded sand hills, where adventurers have frequently been forced to drink the blood of their mules to allay their thirst" in a letter to the editor of the *Missouri Intelligencer* in June, 1825, after the completion of his third expedition to New Mexico.[7] Still, in no extant documents did Becknell recount the incident and Gregg did not record conversing with Becknell during the summer of 1841.[8]

Becknell's failure to mention the incident is puzzling. Perhaps he felt some pangs of embarrassment over being reduced to such a pitiful condition by the forces of nature, or perhaps the incident did not happen to Becknell's party, but to some other group.[9] Whatever occurred on the trail, however, was overshadowed by the greater significance of Becknell's arrival at San Miguel.

Becknell's company rumbled into San Miguel in late July, having announced its presence "with three rounds from our rifles." Members of the expedition "separated at St. Michael for the purpose of trading more advantageously. Some of the company, among whom was Mr. Heath, remained there, and others I did not see again until my return." Some of the newcomers left to trap beaver. According to historian David J. Weber, "two of these, a tall Tennessee carpenter named Ewing Young, and

Kentucky-born William Wolfskill, each in their twenties, began a profitable and lasting relationship which kept them in the vanguard of the Taos trappers."[10]

Becknell sold his merchandise and the goods consigned to him, as well as a wagon he had brought with him from Missouri.[11] He apparently left for Missouri soon after his final sale was made. He may have thought that the route he had recently taken to San Miguel was not the best that could be utilized, for "on our return we took a different course from that pursued on our way out, which considerably shortened the route, and arrived at Fort Osage in 48 days."

The proceeds of William Becknell's second expedition to New Mexico are better defined than those of the first. The *Intelligencer* reported on February 13, 1823:

> We do not doubt that $10,000, or even a much larger sum, was brought into this state during last summer, from Santa Fe, . . . the amount was conveyed upon pack-horses, & c. and not in a waggon [*sic*]. But *one* waggon has ever gone from this state to Santa Fe, and that was taken by Capt. Wm. Becknell, . . . in the early part of last spring, and *sold there* for *seven hundred dollars*, which cost here $150. This information we obtained from Capt. B. personally, who at the same time mentioned his intention of starting again for Santa Fe next fall, with *three* waggons for the same purpose.[12]

The sale of Becknell's wagon alone should have been enough to satisfy any of his remaining debts and perhaps leave him with a generous surplus. Neighbors like Miss Fanny Marshall apparently also enjoyed Becknell's good fortune. William Becknell's industry and daring undoubtedly had won him wealth, fame, and the gratitude of his neighbors. The way was now open to those who would follow his example.

The February 13 edition of the *Intelligencer* also contained a statement that "we are promised by Capt. B. that in a few weeks he will furnish us with such information relative to Santa Fe as will be useful and entertaining to our readers."[13] Becknell must have made good his promise; the result was the appearance of "the journal of Capt. William Becknell" in the *Intelligencer* on April 22, 1823.

Although the entertainment value of the journal was disavowed by the publisher, "information relative to Santa Fe" was included:

> Those who visit the country for the purpose of vending merchandise will do well to take goods of excellent quality and unfaded colors. An idea prevails among the people there, which is certainly a very just one, that the goods hitherto imported into their country, were the remains of old stock, and sometimes damaged. A very great advance is obtained on goods, and the trade is very profitable; money and mules are plentiful, and they do not hesitate to pay the price demanded for an article if it suits their purpose, or their fancy.

Becknell's title of "founder of the Santa Fe trade and father of the Santa Fe Trail" was thus well earned. Through planning and good fortune he had entered the long-forbidden province of New Mexico and found it receptive to trade with the United States. As a determined entrepreneur, he returned to New Mexico further exploiting his success, and in one step raised the status of the trail from a barely discernible wilderness trace to that of a freighting roadway. Becknell was also a publicist, sharing his experiences through an intermediary, thereby reinforcing the desire of others to follow his tracks and encouraging the development of the trail.

The introduction to Becknell's journal prophesied America's westward expansion when it stated:

> The adventurous enterprise and hardy habits of this frontier people [from the United States] will soon penetrate beyond the mountains, compete for trade on the shores of the Pacific, and investigate the advantages of the immense country which extends to the south.

William Becknell would contibute to this process during the next three years.

In October, 1822, when William Becknell returned to Franklin from his second visit to New Mexico,[14] he found that several suits concerning him had been heard in Judge Todd's court during the previous month. On Thursday, September 26, the court heard a complaint against Becknell by Henry E. Dever. The case had been held over from the May term of court, and involved the ownership of a slave. Both parties were represented by their attorneys. A jury found that "the said defendant William Becknell doth not detain the said Slave in the declaration mentioned in manner and form as the said Henry E. Dever hath complained against him." Dever received nothing "for his false clamour" except the privilege of paying the "costs and charges" incurred by Becknell in his defense.[15]

The next suit, also held over from the May term, gave the long-suffering Amos Ashcraft a chance to confront the somewhat elusive William Becknell and James and Jesse Morrison. Judge Todd ruled "that the said defendants did not well and truly pay to the said plaintiff the said sum of money in the declaration," and that "Amos Ashcraft recover against the said William Becknell, James Morrison and Jessee Morrison the said debt of One hundred and twenty dollars and also his damages with his costs and charges. . . ."[16]

Thomas A. Smith also sought redress of grievances against Becknell and the Morrison brothers on the same day. Judge Todd found that "the said defendants did undertake and promise in manner and form as the said plaintiff hath in his declaration complained against them and assess the damages of the said plaintiff by him sustained by reason of the promises to the sum of two hundred and nine dollars ninety six and one third cents."[17] The Boone's Lick saltmakers had experienced a dismal day in court, losing two of two.

Judge Todd also heard an appeal made by William Becknell, Julius Emmons, and Ira Emmons. Becknell and his associates recovered "costs and charges" incurred in earlier litigation with James Rawlings, executor of the estate of John Rawlings, Sr.,[18] but the issue involved in this case is not clear.

The case of the "State of Missouri vs. William Becknell" came before the court in October. Becknell, "here present in Court" acknowledged "himself to owe and stand justly indebted to the state of Missouri in the sum of one hundred dollars. . . ."[19] He had apparently not paid his taxes, although it is unclear whether he was unable to pay or had simply neglected to do so.

After this flurry of litigation, Becknell evidently remained at Franklin until August, 1824, when he set out for a third time for New Mexico. Scant information exists about his activities during the twenty-two-month interim in Missouri. An article appeared in the *Intelligencer* in February, 1823, which recounted the sale of Becknell's wagon in New Mexico on his second trip, and referred to "Capt. B., personally" as the source. Becknell "mentioned his intention of starting again for Santa Fe next fall. . . ."[20] This scheduled departure in 1823 evidently never took place.

Becknell's journal, which appeared in the *Intelligencer* on April 22, 1823, and a few subsequent newspaper notices of letters received at the Franklin post office, provide the only available information about his activities until late summer of 1824.[21] In mid-August Alphonso Wetmore talked to Becknell and learned that he "is about to depart for Santa Fe, accompanied by sixteen men. He intends to visit the Oregon before he returns. He will probably be absent about ten months."[22] Becknell apparently intended to trap his way through the Rockies.[23]

William Becknell's decision to engage in trapping is significant, for his two previous journeys to New Mexico had been made as a merchant. By 1824, however, the New Mexican market was so filled with merchandise from Missouri that trapping offered larger profits to Missouri merchants.[24] Therefore, Becknell joined the vanguard of American trappers entering the Colorado basin.

Becknell made the necessary preparations, likely purchasing some trade goods and almost certainly some traps, and "got off to a late start. His party of sixteen did not leave Franklin, Missouri, until sometime after August 19."[25] This delay would greatly influence the outcome of Becknell's mountain adventure.

No extant accounts describe Becknell's third crossing of the plains to New Mexico, but it is certain that he visited the Governor of New Mexico, Bartolomé Baca, upon his arrival in Santa Fe, and obtained a license to trap in the province. Indeed, one historian suggests that "Becknell may have been the first American to receive a Mexican license to trap."[26]

By November 29, 1824, Becknell was in the village of Santa Cruz, approximately twenty-five miles north of Santa Fe, where he wrote a letter to Governor Baca. "To His Excelannce govirnor of New mexico Bartolar Mr. Barker," Becknell reported, "Seur I have recvd the Lisance you granted me by the onrabel preste [priest] of santa Cruse Manuel Radar and will Comply with your orders and obay them punctaly. Thar is 10 of us to gether all amearican." Becknell planned to spend the winter in the mountains, for he declared that "I shal be in Next June if nothing Hapins to us."[27] He may have thought that seven months would allow him enough time to open a trail to Oregon across the Rocky Mountains; even the best maps available in Becknell's day tended to underestimate the vastness of the Rocky Mountains, the Great Basin, and adjacent western regions.[28]

Becknell's letter assured Baca that "I shal Cum an see you when I Cum in from the woods. The winte[r] is aprochin so near I Cante [find] time to Cum now but all orders from you Shall be apentual [punctually?] obad [obeyed] by me from your oner Seur. Your moste obedante unbil Sarvunte, Capt. Wm. Becknell."[29] The contrast between Becknell's letter to Governor Baca and articles attributed to him in the *Franklin Missouri Intelligencer* emphasizes Becknell's dependence on a literate intermediary.

Becknell left Santa Cruz on November 5, 1824, "with a party of nine men, employed in my service, with a view of trapping on the Green

River, several hundred miles from Santa Fe."[30] He took his men north across rugged terrain, where the land was "poor, and timbered with pine and cedar." The trappers encountered "several tribes of Indians, who were poor and inoffensive." Becknell later learned, however, "that some of the Indians who spent some time with us, afterwards committed murders upon the persons of some of the *engagés* of Mr. Prevost [Etienne Provost], of St. Louis, and robbed the remainder."

The party's November departure provided little time before the rigors of the mountain winter forced them into winter quarters "forty days from settlements." Becknell recalled:

> We suffered every misery incident to such an enterprise in the winter season, such as hunger and cold — but were exempted from robbery. The flesh of a very lean horse, which we were constrained to break our fast with, was, at this time, pronounced excellent. But when his bones were afterwards served up, as a matter of necessity, they were not as well relished, but had nearly proved fatal to the whole party.

Snow was now "three or four feet deep" and the trappers dared not further reduce their supply of horses in quest of nourishment, for, as Becknell's amanuensis put it, "to have eaten them would have been like dining upon our own feet." Instead, the members of the forlorn band "subsisted two days on soup made of a raw hide we had reserved for sealing our moccasins; on the following morning the remains were dished up into a hash." Becknell recalled, perhaps with some irritation, that "the young men employed by me had seen better days, and had never before been supperless to bed nor missed a wholesome and substantial meal at the regular family hour, except one, who was with me when I opened the road to Santa Fe." A bear was subsequently killed and eaten by members of the party with the "table urbanity of a prairie wolf." The scarcity of game made sleep their chief escape from hunger.

During his wanderings from camp, Becknell came upon "old diggings and the remains of furnaces," and "the remains of many small stone houses, some of which have one story beneath the surface of the earth," as well as peices of broken pottery "well baked and neatly painted." His camp, one historian has surmised, may have been "in the area of present-day Mesa Verde National Monument. . . ."[31]

Becknell decided sometime during the first months of 1825 to retreat to the New Mexican pueblos "as the depth of the snow, and the intense cold of the season rendered trapping almost impracticable." Two attempts at breaking through the frozen mountain fastness proved unsuccessful, but a third effort set them on their southeastward course. Along the way, the ragged entourage witnessed the incineration of an elderly Indian woman by members of her own tribe. The sight of this "Hindoo sacrifice" impressed Becknell and "shocked our feelings not a little." The intensity of the mountain winter made life hard for everyone.

Descending from "this inhospitable wilderness," Becknell's party reached a Spanish village on the fifth of April, after an absence of five months. Becknell may have paid his promised visit to Governor Baca in Santa Fe, but his departure from the province was through Taos, well to the north of the provincial capital.

Becknell arrived at Fort Osage, Missouri, in thirty-four days. He had taken a route that "avoided the so much dreaded sand hills, where adventurers have frequently been forced to drink the blood of their mules, to allay their thirst."

The extent of Becknell's profits from his third journey to New Mexico is unclear. On June 11, 1825, the *Intelligencer* reported that Becknell had arrived from New Mexico and that "the company which left this place last summer for the purpose of trapping, have been successful."[32] The article in which Becknell reviewed his latest adventures for readers of the *Intelligencer*, on June 25, 1825, states, however, "although my essays have been unfortunate speculations, I am disposed to make another experiment."[33] The report of June 11 announced that "three or four of the party are reported as missing, and one was killed,"[34] while Becknell's account on June 25 does not mention the loss of any of his employees. Because the *Intelligencer* had published spurious reports of disasters befalling earlier Santa Fe expeditions,[35] Becknell's rendering of June 25 is presumably more accurate, and the monetary rewards of his trapping "experiment" were conceivably disappointing.

Becknell's decision to engage in trapping suggests that he had previous knowledge of what he would later see for himself in New Mexico:

> The trade to this province has been greatly injured by the reduction of prices — while domestics are only fifty cents per yard. An export duty of three per cent, is collected on all specie brought out of the province in this direction.[36]

Although William Becknell's winter expedition of 1824-25 places him in the fraternity of America's legendary Mountain Men, he more accurately qualifies as what historian Richard Hofstadter has termed "the Jacksonian expectant capitalist who 'found conditions that encouraged him to extend himself.'" He was a "hardworking ambitious person for whom enterprise was a kind of religion."[37] When his experiment proved to be an unpromising alternative to the glutted Santa Fe trade, Becknell turned away from trapping much as a gold prospector would abandon the banks of an unproductive stream.

Despite his statement that "I am disposed to make another experiment in trapping," Becknell evidently never returned to the Rocky Mountains of New Mexico. He did, however, contribute to the further development of the trail he had founded. The basis for his continued involvement with the Santa Fe Trail is found in the closing paragraph of his journal: "An excellent road may be made from Fort Osage to Santa Fe. Few places would require much labor to make them passable; and a road might be laid out as not to run more than thirty miles over the mountains."

By 1824, Missourians had come to realize the great benefits inherent in the Mexican trade, and their representatives in Washington were not ignorant of their feelings. This is affirmed by documents of the time.

In August, Alphonso Wetmore, a prominent Missourian, sent a letter to Congressman John Scott in reply to the Congressman's request for information about the Santa Fe Trail. Wetmore recounted the development of the trail, mentioned Becknell's three journeys to New Mexico, the outcome of the third at the time being in question, and cited conversations with "Mr. Becknal [sic]" and Benjamin Cooper, another early participant, as well as the departure of seventy-eight men, "twenty-three carriages, and about two hundred head of horses," in May 1824. He further volunteered that "the most acceptable service that could be rendered those engaged in this inland trade, would be to mark a road, so as to enable them to pursue their operations without loss of time or distance." Wetmore suggested that the United States Army could provide a small number of troops to improve the trail or perhaps twenty to thirty Rangers could be employed for the purpose.[38]

In October, Missouri residents petitioned Congress "for the encouragement of trade and intercourse between Missouri and the Internal Provinces of Mexico," with ample justification of their cause. The petitioners explained that trade with New Mexico was the creation of the industrious citizens of Missouri, and that, with the aid of the government, it would become a lasting and highly profitable contribution to the state of Missouri. The document contained much information about the internal trade routes of Mexico, and portrayed New Mexico as the gateway to other lucrative markets far to the south. Also, with so many American citizens travelling to New Mexico and beyond, the petition suggested, in addition to the monitoring and marking of the trail that there "should be added the authority of consuls in Santa Fe, Chihuahua, and Durango, to guard the rights of their fellow citizens, protect them from impositions, and furnish an official organ of complaint to both governments, in the event of any abuses from the local Mexican authorities."[39]

Perhaps the most famous of these documents concerning the Santa Fe trail is the questionnaire completed by Augustus Storrs, Justice of the Peace at Franklin, at the behest of Senator Thomas Hart Benton of Missouri. Storrs based his replies upon his proximity to the origins of the trail, and his own journey to New Mexico the summer of 1824. Storr's meticulous account of topography, flora and fauna, and revelations of the magnitude of trade, in which he estimated that returns from the trail would "amount to $180,000 . . . principally, in Spanish dollars and bullion" as well as "furs, taken in that country, by Americans, [who] have already returned, amounting by actual sales, to $10,044,"[40] gave abundant reason for the further development of the trail to Santa Fe.

The Missourians found receptive ears in the Congress. Funds were allocated in 1825 for the marking of the Santa Fe Trail, largely through the efforts of Senator Thomas Hart Benton. Historian Robert L. Duffus has summarized Benton's role in colorful language:

> William Becknell is plainly entitled to be called the Trail's father, but to be strictly fair we must give that famous westerner, Senator Thomas Hart Benton, credit for playing the important role of consulting physician both before and after the happy event. As editor, in his youth, of the St. Louis *Inquirer*, Benton had ardently advocated the opening of trade with Mexico across the plains. As a Senator, after the opening of the Mexican frontiers in 1821, he pushed the project with renewed enthusiasm.[41]

In addition to funding the marking of the Santa Fe Trail, Congress entrusted the task to three commissioners: B. H. Reeves, George C. Sibley, and Thomas Mather. Reeves's journal documents William Becknell's participation in the project.

Reeves recorded that on "Wednesday 6th July [I] purchased three Mules of cap Becknel [*sic*] at $40 each," and on "July 8, 1825 — To Cash paid Captn Becknell for 3 Mules pr. order $120.00."[42] Becknell's duties also included bringing mail to and from the expedition, for Reeves noted that he had paid "To cap. Becknel [*sic*] for bearing an express to the commissioners $200," and that he also disbursed to "Wm. Becknell for ferriages and supplies furnished $31.50."[43] According to an entry for February 22, 1826, Reeves paid "of Cap Becknal [sic], who as an express brot [sic] on dispatches to the comrs.,"[44] the sum of two dollars,[45] while on "Dec. 1, 1826 [he] paid Cap Becknell for ferriages & supplies $31.50."[46] Reeves also paid, on January 21, 1826, "To Wm Becknell, For ferriages [of] 5 waggons — 7.50 do [ditto] 22 men and horses — 5.50 for [?] & subsistence — 18.50 [total] $31.50."[47]

William Becknell's participation in the marking of the Santa Fe Trail was far from unimportant, for the commissioners relied upon his knowledge of the route. A member of the party recorded that after rigorous labors west of the Kansas River, the crew

> struck a paper upon a tree with intelligence of Capt. Becknell's having been there on that morning, with some papers from government which we supposed to be instructions: but here we must remain in suspense until he returned as he informs us he will return in a few days. But to the relief of our suspense, and the disappointment of our expectations about 10 o'clock we heard a gun just across the creek from the encampment, at which moment every man sprang to his gun to make ready for action. The night was very dark, but directly he made himself known who proved to be Capt. [Becknell], but no additional instructions; not withstanding there were papers communicated to Col. Reeves; but we think relative to the internal government of our own State. . . . Capt. Becknell informs us that our location is the stream called verdigris [sic]; but we were before informed that none of the tributary streams of that river came from a source as far northward as our road. . . .[48]

The marking party was at times so short of fit draft animals that they were forced to await Becknell's arrival with fresh stock. On Wednesday, October 12, 1825,[49] "Col. Mather, Capt. Becknell, and H. Cooper set out for Fort Osage, to get horses and the two latter to bring them back to us." Nine days later, "in consequence of the reduced state of our horses, Col. Reeves concluded, we had better lie at camp, and await Capt. Becknell's arrival who had not come yet." The company remained idle for only a few hours, for "on this day about 10 o clock to our agreeable surprise Capt. Becknell arrived with his accompanyants, three ewks [sic] of oxen, and 4 horses were brought to our relief."[50] Reeves's account of Friday October 21 states that "about 2 o clock p m H. Cooper Cap Becknal [sic] & [?] Joel Walker met us with a Beef, some salt & a supply of oxen & Horses for the draft, which was a very seasonable relief to us. The exhausted state of our Horses in all probability would have compeld [*sic*] us to have left the waggons [*sic*] & traveled in on foot."[51]

William Becknell's participation in marking the Santa Fe Trail further consolidated his position as "father of the Santa Fe Trail." He took a continued interest in his "offspring," although the remuneration gained in the process probably played a part in his decision. Becknell terminated his activities in the marking venture in December, 1826, perhaps because of another lawsuit,[52] and evidently at that time ended his association with the Santa Fe Trail.

Chapter IV

Becknell's Public Service

Much had changed in Boone's Lick Country since William Becknell's first journey to New Mexico, and the turbid Missouri River was a chief cause. In 1826 the river began to change its course. Becknell's home town of Franklin, which was also home of the *Missouri Intelligencer* and the eastern terminus of the Santa Fe Trail, began to gradually slide into the Missouri.[1] Becknell moved to Arrow Rock township, six miles up river,[2] while the *Intelligencer* moved its offices fifteen miles north to the town of Fayette. Boonville, on a stone bluff directly across the river from Franklin, briefly became the terminus of the Santa Fe Trail. Little remained of Franklin by 1828, and on February 6, 1829, the *Intelligencer* "published the information that it expected the remaining portions of the old town would tumble into the river during that winter."[3]

While the Missouri River carried Franklin downstream piecemeal, boatloads of merchandise destined for New Mexico passed through Boone's Lick Country to discharge their freight far upstream. By 1827, the eastern jumping off point of the Santa Fe Trail had moved to Westport, on Missouri's western border.[4]

Becknell's relocation at Arrow Rock was made with fore-knowledge; he had previously operated a ferry across the Missouri there, perhaps continuing to do so,[5] and had crossed the river there on his expeditions to New Mexico. His prestige served him well, for on June 15, 1827, Governor John Miller of Missouri announced that

> Whereas the County Court of the County of Saline — in the State of Missouri, has recommended William Becknill [*sic*] to be appointed a Justice of the peace, for the Township of Arrow Rock — in the County of Saline, now Therefore, I do here by Commission and said William Becknill [*sic*] as Justice of the peace for the Township and County aforesaid. . .[6]

Becknell took the oath of office on July 12, 1827, in Saline County. Thus encouraged, he successfully sought election to the Missouri House of Representatives the next year, and took his seat there on November 17, 1828. Appropriately, Becknell was placed on the Committee on Public Salines, and subsequently sponsored a bill to amend the state's estray law and a petition to set the boundaries of Saline County. He was also active on bills regulating the militia, County Treasurers, and seminary school lands. The legislative session ended in January, and Becknell returned to Saline County where he engaged in mercantile pursuits.[7] On April 4, 1829, Becknell wrote, with his customary disregard for spelling, to "A. W. Payne, or Brother," residing at "Walnut farm Mo" that

> I can't sell your cotton to any advantage unless I sell it in small quantities and or a creadit I have advertized it to be sold on the last saturday in this month on a creadit of 6 month by giving Note and security for all amount over tow [two] dollars I will have it sold to the best advantage and right you imeadally after if this porposial don not meat youre approbation right directly on the recipt of this but I do not dowbt its selling in this way Eqaley as high as if sold at privet sale. With Respct Sir
>
> > Your OC
> > Wm. Becknell[8]

Meanwhile, Justice of the Peace Becknell carried out his duties in Saline County. An example is found in a letter to Becknell from James Glasgow of neighboring Chariton County, dated July 14, 1829:

> Wm. Becknell Esq.
> > Dear Sir:
> > > Mr. Whitson informs me that Mr. Harris' are willing to pay up the ammount [sic] of the judgement against them in salt. You will please inform them that I will take it in salt delivered to me at this place at 62½ cents per bushel if they will deliver it in two weeks. and inform Mr. Harris it is probable I might trade with him for some more if he wants goods for it.
> > You will attend to having the costs collected.
> >
> > > Yours &
> > > James Glasgow[9]

Such mundane matters were soon swept aside, however, when Major General Stephen Trigg of the First Division Missouri Militia ordered Becknell to muster his Saline Rangers for active duty: Indian problems had intensified in the Osage River basin. On August 8, 1829, Alonzo Pearson, "Generalissimo & Commander in Chief of all the Forces west of the Mississippi River," wrote Captain Becknell explaining that Becknell's Rangers would be the only Saline County company called to serve. He warned that a "rival" Saline County unit, apparently jealous that Becknell's Rangers had been chosen, would be "Scrutinizing into the proceedings of your campaign and may perhaps endeavor to arraign you before me at Head Quarters." Pearson then outlined three "General orders" designed to keep Becknell's boisterous subordinates too busy to cause trouble during their tour of duty.

Becknell was instructed by the first order to establish a camp on the Osage River and then capture as many Indians as could be found within "a considerable distance." These prisoners were to be supplied with skins by Becknell's men and kept "constantly at labor and service" fashioning the skins into articles of clothing for themselves. Pearson warned that Rangers refusing to furnish skins to the Indians would cease to be paid "from that moment," and their clothing replaced by a "Breech cloth" and whatever else they could create to wear Indian style. He further specified that "you will also keep them [the company] at a respectful distance from the Squaws and not even suffer them to look at them except through a noose or a Breech cloth." The Rangers were to practice drill and markmanship so arduously, said order two, "that on your return to head quarters [sic] no man can be found who will be able to compete with them at a Target." Those refusing to participate would lose half their pay.

Pearson's last order was the most curious of the three, and reveals another of William Becknell's many talents: "At all leisure times you will instruct them, at least such as have good eyesight in the science & mystery of Bee hunting, and after having found a sufficient quantity of rich good Honey, select some two or three dozen large hollow trees, with their shells, sycamore if to be found, from 18 to 20 feet round." These trees were to be cut to forty to fifty feet in length, filled with the sticky treasure, and sealed at both ends with beeswax. The Indian captives would then carry or roll these "Osage Bee Gums" to Pearson's headquarters. "You will see that these orders are strictly adhered to by your men," warned the "Generalissimo." Pearson ended his missive with this curious statement, which could only have antagonized Becknell and his men: "My aid S. Martin Esqr. has made but one tour of duty — visiting, consoling & conforting the wives of your men. From accounts he has succeeded to admiration — they think he has more than filled the places of their husbands."[10]

Becknell entered middle age with widespread responsibilities. In 1830, while serving as justice of the peace and member of the Missouri legislature, he was head of a sizable household. His wife Mary was thirty-eight years old, and there were two daughters, one under five and another between ten and fifteen years of age. One of the girls, Cornealia, outlived her father; the other daughter apparently died at an early age. Thirteen-year-old William A. lived with his parents, but John was not living with them. A white woman between sixty and seventy years of age completed the family. Some indication of Becknell's wealth is afforded by the fact that he owned what was evidently a family of slaves: one man between twenty-four and thirty-six, two boys less than two years old, a woman between ten and twenty-four, and one girl under ten years of age.[11]

Becknell sought re-election from Saline County to the Missouri House of Representatives in 1830, and his stance in the campaign indicates that he was politically an ardent Jacksonian. Constitutional amendments had been proposed by Jacksonians in the Missouri legislature that would require the election of circuit court judges, and the 1830 session was to vote on these measures. When elections were held in August, prior to the vote in the House, William Becknell was re-elected "in favor of the amendments,"[12] thus aligning himself with Jacksonians in the legislature.

Representative Becknell spent his second term in the House concerned mainly with salt-related legislation, internal improvements, and a divorce case involving two eminent Missourians; "Generalissimo" Alonzo Pearson and the daughter of Dr. John Sappington, who would soon give the shivering, shaking frontier "Dr. John Sappington's Anti-Fever Pills." On Thursday, December 9, 1830, Becknell moved that the bill annulling the marriage of Pearson and Elizabeth Sappington be sent to committee.[13] On December 24, Becknell wrote Dr. Sappington that "The Bill in relation to your Daughter passed the lower House a few days Since and on yesterday was rejected in the Senate by a vote of 8 to 8 and the presiding officer giving the casting vote against the Bill. . . ."[14] Two days later, Governor John Miller wrote to an interested party that the bill had been tabled and that all that kept it from being passed was Elizabeth Sappington's signature affirming her desire for a divorce. Miller further disclosed that "Capt. Becknell informed me he had written you and enclosed a copy of the bill, which will give you further satisfaction — I should have written to Dr. Sappington but for the delicacy of the matter."[15]

John Sappington, whose medical practice was located at Arrow Rock, was one of Becknell's more illustrious constituents. He had moved to Missouri after practicing medicine in Franklin, Tennessee, for several years and afterward graduating from "a one-year medical course at the University of Pennsylvania."[16] By 1830, the doctor and his wife had eight children and owned twenty-five slaves.[17] Sappington's prominence was enhanced by his successful use of quinine in the treatment of malaria, a frequent scourge along the frontier, and this led in 1832 to the manufacture of "Dr. John Sappington's Anti-Fever Pills." According to one Boone's Lick historian, "his slaves were kept busy compounding the medicine which was composed of one grain quinine, ¾ grain licorice, ½ grain myrrh and oil of sassafras. Patients were instructed to take the medicine every two hours until the symptoms disappeared."[18] Four of Sappington's daughters married future Missouri governors. One of his illustrious sons-in-law was M. M. Marmaduke, who had been a member of Augustus Storr's 1824 expedition to New Mexico.[19] Both Sappington and Marmaduke would influence William Becknell's life at intervals during the next twenty-six years.

By 1832, friction between settlers and Indians had generated warfare in northeastern Illinois, where the recalcitrant chief of the Sauk and Fox Indians, Black Hawk, sought to reoccupy tribal lands. Rumors spread across Missouri that local tribes were planning to join Black Hawk in his "uprising." In August, 1832, a company of militia was organized in Saline County to scour the region to the southwest and assess the attitudes of the Indians there. Forty armed and mounted residents of the county assembled and held the customary election of officers. "Capt. Henry [William] Becknell, who had formerly owned and operated the ferry at Arrow Rock, was chosen captain; Jacob Nave was 1st lieutenant; Ben E. Cooper, 2nd lieutenant; Jackson Smiley, orderly-sergeant."[20]

Militia commander General Stephen Trigg chose Becknell's company as his bodyguard. The militia, "mounting in hot haste," ascended the La Mine and Blackwater rivers between Arrow Rock and Boonville, and in present-day Johnson County swung to the southeast, crossing the Osage River. A supply detail was dispatched to the settlements, and on its return the mission resumed. Numerous Kickapoo war parties were intercepted as they moved to join Black Hawk, and were peacefully convinced to return to their villages. An investigation of Osage camps found no war-like activities.[21]

The militia then returned home. Becknell's company, which had served twenty-one fairly uneventful days, was disbanded upon return to Saline

County. Becknell was not blamed for failure to encounter the enemy. The author of a county history, published forty-nine years later, explained that

> Captain Becknell had been a soldier in the war of 1812, and had seen considerable service. He was also well versed in Indian warfare and fighting, and would have made a good record with his company if he had had opportunities.[22]

William Becknell's activities during the next three years are vague. Apparently, he did not seek re-election to the Missouri legislature in 1832, and his four-year term as Justice of the Peace had expired in 1831. He may have engaged in some form of brokerage, but more plausibly spent much of his time farming.

On January 29, 1834, Becknell and his wife sold two tracts of land to Burton Lawless for the sum of 500 dollars cash. One tract, in Saline County, contained "Seventy-one acres, and Sixty-eight hundriths [*sic*] of an acre, more or less," and another of "Seventy-six acres and seventy-five hundriths of an acre, more or less," located in Howard County.[23] On February 7, 1834, William Becknell bought a slave woman named Phillis, thought to be in her late twenties, and "a male child by the name of Harvey aged about four years. . ." at Lexington in Lafayette County.[24] The Becknell family would influence their lives during the next four decades.[25] Four months later, Mary Becknell acknowledged the sale of property in Cooper County, just east of Saline County. These transactions would seem to indicate some kind of consolidation of assets on William Becknell's part. Such was ultimately the case, for, in the fall of 1835, Captain Becknell led his family and several others southward from Boone's Lick Country,[26] leaving behind a laudable career as one of Missouri's outstanding pioneers.

Chapter V

Becknell Settles in Texas

IN THE CLOSING MONTHS of 1835, William Becknell led his wagon train southward, crossing the Red River into the Mexican province of Texas. Becknell intended to settle in the Anglo-American colonies along the Texas coastal plain, but rumors of hostile Indians caused the caravan to rumble to a halt twenty-five miles south of the river, in present-day Red River County, in the vicinity of the small village of Clarksville. Becknell soon settled on Sulphur Fork Prairie, approximately five miles west of the hamlet.[1] Although residing on Mexican soil, Becknell and his neighbors were largely untouched by Mexico's policies due to the peculiar history of the Red River region.

American settlement in extreme northeast Texas began in June, 1815, when Alex and George Wetmore established a trading post on the Red River at Pecan Point. American communities soon formed at Pecan Point and up river at Jonesborough. Horse thieves traveling from Missouri to Nacogdoches blazed trails through the area. The settlers, thus connected with Missouri, considered themselves under its jurisdiction. The district later became part of Miller County, Arkansas, despite the provisions of the Adams-Onís Treaty of 1819, which clearly placed lands west of th 32nd parallel and south of the Red River under Spanish authority. This anomaly existed until 1836, when Red River area settlers participated in the Texas Revolution as Texans.[2]

The method of settlement in the Red River district contrasted with the more orderly Americanization of Mexican Texas farther south. In 1821 Stephen Fuller Austin, twenty-seven-year-old former member of the Missouri Territorial legislature and district judge in Arkansas, inherited his father's commission from the Spanish government to settle families from the United States in Texas. His liberal land grant for this purpose was reaffirmed by the Mexican government after Mexico gained independence from Spain. Austin was so successful that by 1831, his colony along the lower Brazos and Colorado rivers boasted 5,665 inhabitants. Other colonizers, or empresarios, concurrently brought additional

American settlers into the province, but none matched Austin's success. As early as 1828, Mexican General Manuel Mier y Terán had reported to the general government after a tour of Texas that the North Americans would take control of Texas if action was not taken to compensate for the imbalance. Mexico took numerous steps to alleviate the situation, but the independent-minded Americans bristled at what they considered unnecessary and offensive regulations. The unstable political situation in Mexico, with its frequent changes in government, also frustrated and irritated the colonists.[3]

In 1834, the year before William Becknell moved to Texas, Juan N. Almonte, the Mexican soldier-statesman, visited the province and discovered that the Anglo-Americans and their slaves [Texas was the only Mexican province where slavery was tolerated] comprised roughly four-fifths of the 24,700 inhabitants. The native-born Texans were being smothered by their prolific neighbors from east of the Sabine. The same year saw a more significant development; in April, General Antonio López de Santa Anna assumed control of the Mexican government. He dissolved all forms of representative government in the country and in other ways sought to consolidate his control over the nation. The federalist constitution of Mexico was scrapped and the armies of the self-styled "Napoleon of the West" took to the field, crushing opposition.[4]

The relationship between citizens of Texas and the centralist Mexican government of President Santa Anna reached the breaking point in June, 1835, when a company of Texans under William Barret Travis attacked the Mexican garrison of Anahuac on Galveston Bay. Santa Anna announced the invasion of Texas on August 1, 1835, and began preparing his campaign the following December.

Meanwhile, in October a detachment of Mexican troops had been attacked and routed by a superior Texas force at Gonzales. Within the month, the Texans captured the government supply depot at Goliad and besieged Mexican forces under the command of General Martín Perfecto de Cós, Santa Anna's brother-in-law, at San Antonio. On December 5, 1835, several hundred Texan volunteers stormed into the village and forced General Cós to surrender. Cós and his troops were allowed to leave Texas on the promise that they would never again enter the country as opponents of the Mexican Constitution of 1824; at this point, the Texans were not seeking independence.

A succession of makeshift "governments" sought to coordinate the defense of Texas during the next few months, but by the first weeks of 1836, internal bickering had crippled any cooperative effort to deal with Santa

Anna's approaching sweep through Texas. The arrival of several hundred armed Texas sympathizers from the United States did not compensate for the Texans' lack of preparation; the old mission known as the Alamo fell and on March 27, 1836, approximately 350 recently arrived American volunteers were massacred near Goliad after they had surrendered.

Santa Anna's brutality brought panic to the American settlements along the Texas costal plain. Thousands of Texans left their homes and fled eastward, clinging to the protection of General Sam Houston's growing army. Houston's Fabian retreat ended in southeastern Texas, on a prairie near the San Jacinto River. On April 21 more than 900 ragged, vengeful Texans attacked and routed a Mexican force of between 1,300 and 1,400 veterans under the personal command of Santa Anna. The Mexican president was captured the next day, and Texas's independence, declared the previous March 2, was essentially secured.[5]

As a resident of the distant Red River country, William Becknell was on the periphery of these events, though he was, if accounts of his neighbors are believed, visited by a famous participant in the revolution.

In late 1835 David Crockett, former United States Congressman from Tennessee, crossed the Red River and, with his companions, spent his first night in present-day Texas at the home of John Stiles. There, Crockett stated that

> He was desirous of seeing another friend located in Red River
> County, so Mr. Stiles went with him out to the edge of the
> prairie and pointed out to him the direction across the prairie,
> their being no roads or bridle paths. Thence he and his party of
> three of four men travelled southwest in search of the home of
> William Becknall [sic].[6]

Several area residents, having heard of Crockett's destination, intercepted him on the way to "Becknell's Prairie" and talked with him. Other residents, believing Indian war parties to be west of Clarksville, trailed Crockett to Becknell's home and warned him to take a more easterly course into Texas. Crockett and his associates stayed at Becknell's "for a few days waiting for recruits to escort them on to join Houston's Army or Colonel Travis at San Antonio," and then rode east on their fateful course into Texas.[7]

In March or April, 1836, President David G. Burnet of the Republic of Texas issued a proclamation "To the Citizens of Texas Residing in the Municipality of Red River" stating that

The enemy is advancing upon your brothers, their hands still warm with the blood of our gallant brothers slaughtered in the Alamo. In the name of Texas, I exhort you citizens of Red River to repair with alacrity to the field, and chastise the audacity of the invaders. . . . Your all is at stake, your wives, your children, all that is dear and sacred to freemen summon you to the field. Your inherent gallantry will promptly obey the call.[8]

From their first days on the Sulphur Fork Prairie, Becknell and his neighbors had organized for defense against expected Indian attack.[9] Insulated by geography from Santa Anna's advance, they were still anxious about the intentions of their Indian neighbors. The possibility that the Indians would take advantage of the havoc caused by the Mexican offensive may have troubled them. Accordingly, on April 28 a constitution for the government of a company of Red River volunteers was drafted and William Becknell was chosen as its captain. The purpose of the unit was "to guarde [sic] the North Western boundary of Texas, to the Sabine and Trinity Rivers." Among Becknell's men was First Lieutenant Thomas Hill, Second Lieutenant B. J. Jeffers, First Sergeant Mansel W. Matthews, and Second Sergeant J. C. Smiley. His sons, William A. Becknell and John C. Becknell, were two of the forty-four privates in the company, but they were absent "on business" during the unit's one month of service.[10]

On May 28, Becknell wrote a letter to General Sam Houston from the Red River settlement of Pecan Point. Becknell introduced himself, gave a synopsis of his months in Texas, reviewed the Indian problems on the northeastern frontier, and volunteered his company for construction of a "Foart on the Watters of the Sabine and Trinity."[11] Unknown to the veteran fort builder, Houston was in New Orleans being treated for an ankle wound suffered on April 21 during the Battle of San Jacinto. The letter found its way to disputatious Brigadier General Thomas Jefferson Green, who responded:

. . . I have to say that your service is much wanted at present. The Mexicans with a much larger army than ours is upon our southern frontier and fast advancing upon our country. The Indians upon our northern border in hostile array. Under this situation no friend of this country will stay at home.

. . . If this dispatch should reach you up Red River it will be more convenient & nearer for you to come through the Indian Country & give me as much protection to the people upon your route as circumstances will permit. If you can engage the hostile Indians to advantage, do so & give them a most exemplary punishment. In doing this you will delay as little time as possible in reaching headquarters of the army & bring on all the volunteers in your reach.

Much reliance is placed in your experience & knowledge of Indian character, so we have no serious fears that you will be supprised [sic] at any time by them.[12]

General Green's communication, dated June 25, led to a meeting at James Clark's house on Sulphur Fork Prairie, where William Becknell organized a new company of volunteers on July 14. It was decided that the unit would be known as the Red River Blues, and Becknell was elected its captain. James Clark, the founder of Clarksville, was chosen Becknell's second in command. In total, the company consisted of three commissioned officers, seven noncommissioned officers, fifty-five privates, one musician, and one company surgeon.[13]

The Red River Blues started south on July 17, leaving fourteen members behind because of illness or unfinished business. Four days later the company was on the banks of the Sabine River, and Sergeant Smiley and one private were sent back to the Sulphur Fork Prairie to collect the fourteen men who had been left behind. By July 30 they had reached Nacogdoches, where a recruit was added to the muster roll. The company then rode through the pine forests on a southwesterly course. Along the way Sergeant William H. Hopkins and one private were so ill that they and two guards had to be left at "White's 25 miles E of the Trinidad," on August 4. The "Trinidad," or Trinity River, was crossed at Nathaniel Robbin's Ferry four days later.[14] Sickness again caused delay within a few days when Lietenant Clark and eight enlisted men were left at "Cow Cooper's old place on Mill Creek;"[15] seventeen-year-old Private John Roland died on August 21.

Becknell's expedition had thus far been uneventful, except for the apparent epidemic that tormented the company. Caddo, Shawnee, and Cherokee lands had been crossed with little more than a rumor than twenty to twenty-five Caddoes were marauding in regions unknown.

By August 26 the Red River Blues were "3 miles above Victoria," approximately thirty miles from the Texas Gulf coast. The first week in September found Becknell and his men stationed, with two other Red River area units,[16] at Camp Johnson, near "Dimmitt's Landing" on the lower Lavaca River.[17] It was there that General Green sent orders to "Capt. Becknell, Texas Army," on September 7:

> You will proceed forthwith up the La Bacca [*sic*] river in pursuit of John Hallet, and his accomplices a notorious thief and villain who it is represented has been for some time stealing horses and cattle & c.

> You will carry with you such of your company as are well enough to do duty after leaving a detail of men to take care of your sick & baggage. Each man will carry six days rations with him. When you overhaul this banditti or any other in your route if they make any resistance shoot the whole of them, otherwise secure them with strings or irons and bring them to camp with such plunder as you may find up[on] them & also all the live stock of any kind. Your men will be allowed each one dollar per day while driving in the stock. The gentlemen who will be with you as pilots is to be allowed for their trouble a horse each out of the captured. Understandings from here say that Capt. Southerland has gone upon the same business with his company, you will if you meet with him cooperate in this object.

> You should also keep a lookout should any Indians be in your route and attack them to the best advantage.

> You are also entitled to use such beef and bread upon your route as will be necessary for your men, taking care to mention the brands of the cattle so taken and reciepting [*sic*] for the corn.

> In the discharge of these duties viligence [*sic*] & perservance [*sic*] is expected of one of your great experience.[18]

Becknell had approximately thirty men able to serve in the campaign Green had assigned, although he probably took fewer with him owing to the illness in camp and the men needed to aid the sick and guard the company's baggage. By September 13 Becknell's mission was completed, and he dictated the following report to his commander:

Camp Dimmitt Sept. the 13th 1836

Genl Green Dr Sir

We proceeded to the upper settlement on the La Bacca [*sic*].
Capt. Southerland had arrived there one day before we did
and had taken possession of all the Horses, and did not wish to
Cooperate with me as I was not there as soon as he was: I
found John Hallet and brought him in, I found no Publick [*sic*]
property with him but his neighbours say he has a Passport in
Spanish assigned by Santiana [*sic*] and sealed accordingly —
We got no Cattle There was no Beef and but few Cows and
Calves which were left with the Settlers by orders of Capt.
Southerland, which prevented us from fetching two or three
Rascals who had the Horses —

Wm Becknall [*sic*] Capt,

Sgt.[?]Adam Zumault [Zumwalt]

will Testify that he has seen the passport of Hallet who read
it to him[19]

Zumwalt's participation in the Hallet incident suggests that Becknell
had renewed old friendships in the region. Empresario Green De Witt,
formerly of Missouri, had attracted many Missourians to his grant along
the Guadalupe, San Marcos, and Lavaca rivers before the revolution.
Zumwalt, not a member of the Red River Blues, had served in James
Callaway's company in 1812 and 1813, as had another area resident,
Jacob C. Darst. The Zumwalts maintained a fort in St. Charles County
during the War of 1812, and Daniel Morgan Boone's own fort was located
in Darst's Bottom, St. Charles County.[20] Therefore, Becknell's tour of
duty in the Lavaca basin may have been more pleasant than evidences of
disease and dealings with military dilletantes would indicate. Indeed,
Becknell probably began his pursuit of the outlaw Hallet secure in the
knowledge that its successful outcome would add luster to a triumph at
Camp Johnson a few days before he ascended the Lavaca River.

Elections for officials of the Republic of Texas had been held on
September 5, 1836, at the behest of the hardpressed *ad interim* government. Texans voted for candidates seeking the offices of president, vice
president, senator, and representative, and residents of the various
precincts serving in the army were allowed to vote at their stations. The
Red River region was alloted three seats in the House of Representatives,
and William Becknell, on duty far to the south, was one of the
candidates.[21]

Eighty Red River volunteers, composed of Becknell's and Hart's companies, cast their votes at Dimmitt's Landing. The results were tabulated in the Red River settlements, and the constituents stationed on the Lavaca River could only assume the outcome. William Becknell, Private Mansell W. Matthews of Becknell's company, and First Lieutenant George W. Wright of Hart's company, having received the majority of votes from the Red River troops, confidently made arrangements to leave their posts and take their places at the first session of Congress, scheduled to assemble October 3, 1836, at Columbia. Captain Becknell turned command of the Red River Blues over to Lieutenant James Clark,[22] and with Matthews and Wright, traveled approximately seventy miles northeast to Columbia, on the Brazos River.

On Monday, October 3, William Becknell presented his credentials to the House of Representatives, and took his seat as a duly elected representative of the Red River district.[23] The next day, "the house met, pursuant to adjourment at ten o'clock and on motion of Mr. Baker and Mr. Becknell, the oaths of office were administered to the sergeant-at-arms, doorkeeper, and engrossing clerk." At two o'clock the next afternoon, "on motion of Mr. Becknell, the house then adjourned until ten o'clock the following day."[24]

William Becknell's tenure in the Congress of the Republic of Texas was short-lived, for seventy-year-old Collin McKinney soon arrived at Columbia with the final count of votes cast by residents of the Red River region, both at home and on duty at Camp Johnson. McKinney had received 169 votes, Wright garnered 156 votes, Matthews had 143 votes, and Becknell 133. Five other candidates, including Lieutenant Clark and Captain Hart, had received substantially fewer votes.[25]

On Wednesday, October 12, the chairman of the committee on privileges and elections, Sidney O. Pennington, reported to the House that:

> . . . after an examination of the polls from the Red River
> County, to us returned, that Messrs. Matthews, Wright and
> M'Kinny [sic], are members elect from Red River; the said
> members having received the highest number of votes of said
> county, and your committee is of the opinion that Collin
> M'Kinny should be allowed to take his seat as a member of the
> House of Representatives.[26]

A motion to adopt Pennington's report was rejected by the members of the House, and the meeting was adjourned until that evening. At an

evening session, however, as one historian has explained, "Becknell himself moved that the report of the committee be reconsidered, and, after a
favorable vote, he generously moved its adoption. The House having
voted affirmatively upon Becknell's motion, McKinney was seated."[27]

Becknell received a certificate of service and a statement of mileage
from the clerk, but Pennington "objected to the payment of mileage as in
the event of three or four members contesting a seat, the country would be
taxed with the traveling expenses of all." General Thomas Jefferson
Green, former member of the North Carolina and Florida legislatures,
Becknell's former commanding officer, and representative from Bexar
County, stated that a certificate signed by judges authorized to hold elections was, in his opinion, "sufficient justification for any man to present
himself to this house; and he considered that the mileage ought to be
allowed." Becknell was allowed to keep the treasury certificates.[28]

The Red River Blues left government service the next day, October 14,
and conceivably departed the Lavaca Bay area en masse shortly
thereafter.[29] By November 4, eleven members of Becknell's company had
visited the office of Auditor of the Republic Asa Brigham, "presenting to
this office claims for horses and other property lost in service. . . ." All
eleven were listed together as "Members of Capt. W. Becknell's
Company" in a letter from Brigham to the Secretary of the Treasury.[30]
The unit returned to Red River County after two months and fourteen
days in the service of the Republic.[31]

Meanwhile, Becknell was a week or more ahead of his former subordinates on the northward trail to the Red River region. His thoughts may
have turned to his brief but active hours in the Congress, and the support
given him by General Green. As so often in the past, Becknell's agile mind
was formulating a plan that might again allow him to serve his adopted
country. Accordingly, at Fort Bend on October 18, 1836, just a few days
into his journey home, Becknell penned a very awkward note to Green:

> Dear Sir
>   After my respects to you if should make [a regiment ?] of
> Carelear [Cavaliers] if you thinke me worthy of your notes you
> will [make use ?] of my Name as a candidate to Command the
> Northern parte of that Corps and send me the Bill and I will
> operate on it and oblige your old friend
>
>   Wm. Becknell[32]

By November 4, Becknell had arrived in Nacogdoches, where he pro-
duced a much more lucid letter to General Green:

Hon. Thos. J. Green
Dear Sir:

I am this far on my way in good health. I hope I shall be able to get Home in a few days and shall in a short time after proceed with my Company of Old Rangers on the Anticipated excursion we spoke of when I saw you and report to you so soon as I return. My present opinion is that there had better be some fortifications at or near the three forks of the Trinity but of this I will inform you more particularly when I make you my report. Should the Government conclude to do so I am willing to take the Command as respects this Station. — I wish you to inform me pr. the Hon. G. W. Wright the particulars of the acts of Congress and also relating to myself and the Section of Country in which I live.

With sentiments of high respect I am yours

Respectfully
Wm. Becknell[33]

Despite his requests, Becknell was not authorized to build a fort in the vicinity of present-day Dallas. Newly-elected President Sam Houston was determined to avoid renewed hostilities with Indians and reduce the size of the often unruly military. General Green, occupied with more urgent matters, evidently failed to promote Becknell's plan, and the three forks of the Trinity had to await the construction of an army outpost until 1841.[34]

Becknell apparently spent the next two years farming on Becknell's Prairie, assisted by his sons William A. and John, and his slaves. They must have kept their firearms close by as they performed their tasks, for by 1837 uneasy relations between settlers and Indians had degenerated into open warfare.

The conflict in the Red River region was atypical because both settlers and Indians were immigrants. Shawnees, Delawares, Cherokees, and Kickapoos, among others, had been overtaken by waves of Americans settling among them and had moved as refugees from the United States to northeast Texas. The Caddoes, ancient residents of Louisiana and East Texas, had also left their tribal lands to make new homes in northeast Texas. These agricultural tribes settled south and west of the Red River district on the headwaters of the Sabine River, where they took possession of the richest lands. But these Indians were again overtaken by groups of American settlers who quickly discerned that the most desirable farm lands had been taken.[35] Conflict soon developed.

On May 15, 1837, a party of settlers under Daniel Montague raided a village of Cherokees, Kickapoos, Shawnees, and Delawares in present Fannin County, some fifty miles west of Clarksville. Several Indians were killed and their bodies burned while surviving tribesmen in the area were herded together and induced to pledge peace. By the next fall, however, Indians were making predatory visits to the Red River settlements.[36]

The settlers of northeast Texas looked to General John H. Dyer, commander of the Fourth Militia Brigade headquartered at Clarksville, for assistance. Clarksville served this purpose because Dyer, whose office was elective, lived there. Dyer organized ranging companies which scoured areas frequented by Indian raiding parties. These units repaired several civilian "forts" across northeast Texas and helped mobilize civilian defense,[37] but the killing and looting continued.

William Becknell organized a militia company in 1838. Many members had served in the Red River Blues two years earlier, and had found in the interim that their tour of duty in 1836 did not meet the Land Office minimum of three months' service for receiving bounty land certificates. Becknell, having commanded the local defense company prior to forming the Red River Blues, had qualified for a 320-acre land certificate in December, 1837, and was well on his way toward a second certificate. It was decided that all would benefit from a two-week tour of duty, and accordingly, fourteen days were served.[38]

Becknell's unit was evidently not one of the far-ranging companies formed by General Dyer prior to November, 1838. They may have participated at some point in Dyer's campaign to the three forks of the Trinity, in which several hundred militia men participated, from November 24, 1838, to January, 1839,[39] but their two-week tour of duty suggests Becknell's company did not venture far from Clarksville.

Becknell and his family apparently prospered during subsequent years. Both his sons had reached voting age by at least 1838, and John was taxed for three slaves that year.[40] William A. Becknell sold one-third of a league of land to Martin Guest in March of that year for $2,000, and a few months later John sold 300 acres of "good tilable land" in Red River County to B. F. Ellis.[41] The 1840 census indicates their father claimed 3,500 acres "under [a] survey based on a grant, but without a final title confirmed by the General Land Office," and that John C. Becknell owned three slaves and three horses,[42] but no land. William Becknell evidently sold 1,656 acres sometime in 1841, for the tax rolls for that year showed he claimed 3,344 acres.[43]

But the "Father of the Santa Fe Trade" had not settled down to the quiet life of a country squire. In March, 1840, William Becknell and son John were prosecuted for assault and battery by Williams Dish, attorney for the Republic of Texas, but the case was dismissed. The elder Becknell was sued during the same month for a $125 debt by Charles E. Spencer and found guilty by a jury including A. H. Latimer and John Stiles, former members of the Red River Blues.[44]

Captain Becknell served his last tour of military duty, a total of ninety days, between June 26, 1841, and June 26, 1842. Although this was the time of the Texas Santa Fe Expedition, and the capture of Refugio, San Antonio, and Goliad by an invading Mexican army, Becknell's activities were evidently confined to Red River County.[45]

By 1843 William Becknell claimed only 2,344 acres in Red River County, compared to the 3,344 acres claimed in 1841.[46] That Becknell declared exactly 1,000 fewer acres may have been his acknowledgement of a debt owed to Dr. John Sappington of Missouri, and the basis of a Red River County folk legend. This legend, that a local farmer traded 1,000 acres of rich farm land for a few thousand anti-fever pills, is founded upon the Becknell-Sappington transaction. Its origin was in Missouri, at least as early as December, 1830, when Representative Becknell and Dr. Sappington cooperated in obtaining the divorce of Sappington's daughter from Alonzo Pearson.

Sappington's records indicate that Becknell owed him money at that time . . . $2.87½, and another $4.37½, loaned between 1830 and 1832. The latter debt was due November 27, 1832. Several other debts of like amounts were owed by Becknell until October, 1834. These charges may have been made for medical treatment, but since Becknell owed $4.37½ to "Sappington and George Penn,"[47] Sappington's associate in the quinine pill business,[48] the purchase of quinine pills probably incurred the debts. Becknell's relatively small purchases suggest that he bought the pills for his family's use and not for resale.

Dr. Sappington's pills enjoyed great success along the western frontier. He sent out distributors and advertised widely.[49] According to Red River County legend, when Sappington's business interests brought him to Clarksville in 1838, he naturally sought out the residence of Captain William Becknell. Sappington's desire to see his former Arrow Rock neighbor, legislator, and customer led to a visit during which Becknell gave him a note in exchange for $2,000 worth of Sappington's Pills. Sappington eventually realized that Becknell could not satisfy the note, and a lawsuit followed in which Becknell lost 1,000 acres of land.[50]

In fact, however, Becknell reported to Sappington in a letter dated September 12, 1840, that Peter Ringo, one of Sappington's traveling salesmen,[51] sold him a supply of pills and "promised to make no other deposit neare [sic] me — But I soon found the Country stocked with them which disapointed [sic] me in making sale of what I had." In desperation, Becknell "packed them out to the interiour [interior of the Republic of Texas] and sold them for Texas mony [sic] which I will pay you in with pleasure, or in good land at a reasonable price." It was the best Becknell could do, for "gold or silver Can not be had at this time in Texas."[52] These alternatives must have troubled Dr. Sappington; Texas currency was worth little in the United States,[53] and ownership of land in Texas was restricted to citizens of the Republic. Sappington's dilemma was not quickly solved.

By 1844 Sappington had given the note to his son-in-law, former Governor M. M. Marmaduke, who notified Thomas J. Shannon, his agent in Texas, to pursue the matter. Shannon also found that Becknell could not pay the note, but had sufficient land to satisfy the debt. Because Marmaduke was not a resident of the Republic of Texas, he could not own land there, but he authorized Shannon to take possession of the land as his agent.[54] Thomas Weight presented himself to Becknell and told him that he was to satisfy the note by transferring title to 1,000 acres to Shannon. In Becknell's words:

> There were two reasons given why the Deed was to be made to Shannon — Thomas C. Weight the agant [sic] of Dr. John Sappington was at my House at the time the Bond for Title to said land was made to Shannon; and said to me that He (Weight) was willing to give me up my note of Two Thousand Dollars, and take the Land which proposition I accepted, and it was then agreed among the parties that I should make a Deed to Thomas J. Shannon, and I accordingly gave my bond for that purpose.[55]

Becknell's compliance with Weight's request was unfortunate, for Weight and Shannon did not report the transaction to Marmaduke or Sappington. Instead, Shannon sold the land to his brother James. Marmaduke eventually learned of this treachery and filed suit against Thomas Shannon and William Becknell. Becknell had not, however, transferred title to the 1,000 acres to Shannon, and the Supreme Court of the State of Texas awarded Marmaduke the land in 1855.[56] Dr. Sappington died on September 7, 1856; engraved on one side of his vault, at his request, was the inscription, "A truly honest man is the noblest work of God."[57]

Notwithstanding his misfortune with Dr. Sappington, Becknell continued to prosper in Texas. Tax records show that in 1843 his holdings consisted of two work horses, 2,344 acres of land, three slaves over ten years of age, and one slave less than ten years old. Martin, the oldest of the four, was forty-nine in that year. Phillis, an epileptic, and her son Harve were forty-one and thirteen years old, respectively. Young Martin, under ten years of age, was evidently the son of Martin and Phillis, although Harve, purchased in Missouri by Becknell in 1834 with Phillis, may have had a different father.[58] Becknell also owned 1,030 acres in neighboring Lamar County. In 1844 he acquired five "town lots," perhaps in Clarksville. By 1845, Becknell's herds had grown to 215 head of cattle and thirty-nine horses; the cattle were marked with an "upper half crop and underbit" cut into the right ear, and an "under half crop in the left ear," with a B burned into the left hip.[59]

By this time Becknell was evidently an active cattle broker as well as a stock raiser. In September, 1849, he wrote United States Senator Thomas J. Rusk an enlightening, if ungrammatical letter concerning a particularly troublesome transaction:

Dear Genrl.

I have concluded to send my son to Nacogdoches to see you in regaurd to the small settlement remaining between us. I sent Conl. Warren to Smith. He told him the cattle ware soald and he purchesed them and wowld not give them up. The order is credeted on the ricept. I wish you to be so good as to take the order and settle with me, as I never can be able to ride on horseback. In 1 [12 ?] former letters I informed you of the missfortune which has rendered me an intire cripple for life, and this induces me to send my papers to you by my son. You are well accqwainted with all the transactions concerning them and I wish you to have the goodness to settle it for me and send me as much money as you can and also pay your self for your troble that you have had at diferent times in attending to this busniss for me. I am compeld to call on you at this time to procure mony to licqwadate my Dr. bills and some other debt which my sitwation reqwired to make at that Time. I wish if possible, to have a final settlement of this bwisness so I can pay my small accounts and I may never have an opertunety of sending to you again by any safe hand. Please present my respects to Mrs. Rusk and family, Youre friend

Wm. Becknell[60]

By 1850 Becknell had acquired a bridge in addition to his other properties. The 1850 census shows that William Becknell was a farmer with $3,000 worth of real estate, plus a bridge spanning the Sulphur River, connecting Red River and Titus Counties.[61] Charles De Morse, editor of the Clarksville *Standard*, described a journey from Mt. Pleasant, Titus County, to Clarksville in March, 1854, which took him over that bridge.

> On Sunday last, the traveling company composed of the District Judge, District Attorney, sundry legal gentleman, a certain editor of a paper in Northern Texas [De Morse], and some chance companions, started for Becknell's Bridge over the Sulphur [the southern boundary between Red River and Titus Counties] . . . . We arrived at the hospitable roof of Capt. Becknell, in the edge of the White Oak timber, before sun down very much fatigued, and partook of the palatable meal set before us, with a gusto that the quiet dweller at home seldom knows.[62]

Becknell's operation of both "Becknell's Prairie" in central Red River County and the bridge across the Sulphur River on the southern edge of the county, may have been a family cooperative.

Toward the end of his life, on February 28, 1852, Becknell's fortunes increased still further, when the Fourth Legislature of the State of Texas belatedly passed a "joint resolution for the relief of the company of Rangers commanded by Captain William Becknell in the year 1836."[63] This news brought a flurry of newspaper notices concerning lost discharges. On August 21, 1852, William A. Becknell, John C. Becknell, Isaac Guest, Jordan P. Ward and Shem Harris advised the community via the Clarksville *Northern Standard*, that unless their discharges from Becknell's company of Rangers were found, they would "apply at the proper office for duplicates."[64] Samuel Jeffus, Johnson Jeffus, David Bawgle, and John Bloodworth jointly gave like notice on October 16, followed by Richard Tankersly on March 5, 1853, and interested parties seeking the discharges of A. C. C. Baily and Joseph J. Guest in December, 1853.[65]

William Becknell and his sons were issued land certificates once their claims were verified. Becknell received one league (4,428 acres), and one labor (177 acres) in Red River County. William A. Becknell was awarded one-third of a league in Red River County and John C. Becknell at least that much and perhaps as much as his father. The three Becknells also received 320 acres each in land bounty warrants some time prior to August 1, 1856.[66]

Becknell was politically less active in the last two decades of his life than he had been previously. On two occasions, however, he served as a precinct judge in Red River County. By appointment of Chief Justice William H. Stout, Becknell supervised the Texas Congressional election at Henry Dufy's residence in September, 1845. In March, 1846, after Texas's annexation, Becknell supervised balloting for United States Congressman at the same location.[67]

William Becknell died April 25, 1856, at the age of sixty-eight. The *Clarksville Standard* contained the following notice:

Died

At his residence in this County on yesterday evening, at an advanced age, Capt. William Becknell.

The above announcement will cause feelings of regret to the first settlers of this County, as well as all acquainted with the deceased.

Capt. Becknell was the first that crossed the plains to Santa Fe — was elected Captain of the first Company that was formed in Northern Texas in 1836 and while in the Military service was elected Representative to Congress. Though his old age exempted him from military service, he was present and participated in most of the battles of the Country. "The old man eloquent" delighted till the close of his life, to relate the events connected with the first settlement of Missouri, California, and more especially his last adopted [?] Country, to the numerous participants of his hospitality. We knew Capt. Becknell well for many years. He was a man of decided character, great _____ [?] and firmness — a model of a pioneer, _____ [?]of the first trip to Santa Fe, was full of incident and suffering. His name appears various places in the Statutes of Texas _____ [as?] a Captain of Rangers. Long before this in the War of 1812, and in the Black Hawk War, we believe he did stout service. The old pioneer is gone, peace to his ashes![68]

Although Editor Charles De Morse's eulogy affords a rare summary of Becknell's achievements, observations by a former neighbor in Missouri describes, perhaps with awe, the rugged character of the adventurous Captain:

> He was not of a religious turn of mind at all. Capt. B. was not.
> Many a settler remembers how volubly and with what
> wonderful force and power he could swear. He was a rough-
> and-tumble fighter of no mean ability.[69]

Becknell died intestate, leaving property worth $12,615. The major
portion of the estate was land: 2,705 acres on Becknell's Prairie valued at
$8,115, 900 acres of unlocated land in land certificates amounting to
$450, and 160 acres held by bounty warrant valued at $136. Becknell's
four slaves, Harve, Martin, young Martin and Phillis, were the next
largest portion of the estate; $2,600. Miscellaneous livestock and farm im-
plements comprised the remainder of the estate.[70]

William Becknell was buried on a rise in Becknell's Prairie. Mary
Becknell stated in her will, executed October 7, 1862, that

> I wish a monument put over Mr. Becknell's grave worth fifty
> dollars with this inscription, Capt. Wm. Becknell, Born in the
> State of Virginia Amhurst Co. died in the State of Texas Red
> River County, on the 30th day of April A.D. 1856, aged sixty-
> eight years. He whose merit deserves a Temple can scarce find
> a tomb.[71]

The location of Becknell's grave was eventually forgotten after Mary
Becknell's death in 1864.[72] By 1957, however, the grave was located and
marked with a large gray granite stone provided by the State of Texas. It
stands approximately five miles west of Clarksville in a cattle pasture,
some two hundred yards south of United States Highway 82. A small
grove of trees beside the grave provides droves of cattle with relief form
the blazing summer sun. Mary Becknell's lament comes readily to mind.

William Becknell's resting place is analogous to his role in American
history: As "founder of the Santa Fe trade and father of the Santa Fe
Trail," he warrants a stone marker recalling his greatest achievement;[73] its
seclusion emphasizes that William Becknell was one of many thousands
who opened the West and now lie buried in forgotten places.

NOTES

Chapter I. A Fortune Made and Lost

1. Becknell is awarded this accolade in Ray Allen Billington's *Westward Expansion*, as well as the title "founder of the Santa Fe trade and father of the Santa Fe Trail" in various other works. Ray Allen Billington, *Westward Expansion* 3rd ed. (New York: Macmillan Company, 1967), p. 463. See also, e.g., Walter Williams and Floyd C. Shoemaker, *Missouri, Mother of the West*, 5 vols. (Chicago: The American Historical Society, Inc., 1930), 1:583.

2. Will of Mary Becknell, Book B. Red River County Court House, Texas, p. 61. Also, Bailey F. Davis to Rex W. Strickland, El Paso, 10 November, 1971, Personal Files of Rex W. Strickland, El Paso, Texas.

3. William Armstrong Crozier, ed., *Virginia Colonial Militia 1651-1776* (Baltimore: Southern Book Co., 1954), p. 67.

4. Davis to Strickland, 10 November 1971.

5. Bailey Fulton Davis, *Amherst County, Virginia, Will Books 1761-1919, B Section* (Amherst Courthouse, Virginia: By the Author, 1962), p. 22.

6. Davis to Strickland, 10 November 1971.

7. Davis, *Will Books 1761-1919*, p. 22.

8. William Montgomery Sweeny, *Marriage Bonds and other Marriage Records of Amherst County, Virginia 1763-1800* (Lynchburg: J. P. Bell Company, 1937), p. 8.

9. Interview with Rex W. Strickland, Professor Emeritus of History, The University of Texas at El Paso, El Paso, Texas, 27 December 1979.

10. Personal Files of Rex W. Strickland, El Paso, Texas; Davis to Strickland, 10 November 1971; Becknell would be influenced by the actions of both men's families during his lifetime. Missouri soon possessed a remarkable abundance of such illustrious pioneers.

11. Bailey F. Davis to Rex W. Strickland, El Paso, 9 November 1971, Personal Files of Rex W. Strickland, El Paso, Texas.

12. At least one person sought to contact Becknell by letter at St. Louis. *St. Louis Louisiana Gazette*, 3 May 1810, p. 3.

13. Eugene Morrow Violette, *A History of Missouri* (Cape Girardeau: Ramfre Press, 1951), p. 68.

14. Homer De Golyer notes from St. Charles Circuit Court Records, Book A, pp. 104, 181; County Deed Record Book E, p. 260. Homer De Golyer Becknell Collection, De Golyer Library, Fikes Hall of Special Collections, Southern Methodist University (hereinafter cited as HDBC).

15. Violette, *History of Missouri*, p. 66-68.

16. Susie Smith Vandiver, "Social and Cultural History of St. Louis During the War of 1812" (M.A. thesis, Southern Methodist University, 1954), p. vi.

17. Frederic L. Billon, *Annals of St. Louis in its Territorial Days* (St. Louis: Nexon-Jones Printing Co., 1880), pp. 412-413.

18. *Kansas City Times*, 30 August 1960, p. 5. See also, Henry C. Levens and N. M. Drake, *History of Cooper County* (n.p.), pp. 13-14.

19. Edgar B. Wesley, "James Callaway in the War of 1812; Letters, Diary, and Rosters," *Missouri Historical Society Collections*, 5 (October 1927): p. 49.

20. Becknell declared in his Bounty Land Claim of May 30, 1853 only that he had been an Orderly Sergeant in Boone's Company, although his service record indicates that he was First Sergeant. Becknell was a non-commissioned officer nevertheless. National Archives (G.S.A.), Military Service Records (N.N.C.S.), William Becknell. Rangers, U.S. Mounted Volunteers (War of 1812), Washington, D.C. Photocopies from Personal Files of Rex W. Strickland, El Paso, Texas. Hereinafter cited as MSRB.

21. Floyd C. Shoemaker, ed., "Missouri Forts in the War of 1812," *Missouri Historical Review* 26 (April 1932): p. 285.

22. On September 24, 1814, Callaway wrote his wife about Fort Johnson, which he and his men had just completed: "we have our fort finished and it is verry [sic] Strong." He also drew a detailed map of the fort. Wesley, "James Callaway," pp 50, 72.

23. *Ibid.*, pp. 50, 45.

24. MSRB, 31 August 1813; 31 October 1813.

25. Wesley, "James Callaway," p. 50.

26. *Ibid.*, pp. 50, 59; see also MSRB 31 December 1813.

27. Shoemaker, "Missouri Forts," p. 288.

28. Wesley, "James Callaway," pp. 59-60.

29. Shoemaker, "Missouri Forts," p. 288.

30. MSRB, 31 December 1813; 28 February 1814; 30 April 1814.

31. Wesley, "James Callaway," pp. 61-62.

32. Kate L. Gregg, "The War of 1812 on the Missouri Frontier," *Missouri Historical Review* 33 (October 1938-July 1939): pp. 327-328

33. Wesley, "James Callaway," pp. 61, 63

34. MSRB, 30 June 1814; see also National Archives (B.S.A.), Bounty Land Claims, War of 1812, William Becknell BLWT 25927-160-50.

35. Stout's Fort was located one mile south of present-day Auburn, Lincoln County, Missouri. Shoemaker, "Missouri Forts," p. 285; and MSRB, 30 June 1814.

36. Wesley, "James Callaway," pp. 63-65.

37. HDBC; MSRB, 30 June 1814.

38. Wesley, "James Callaway," pp. 65-66.

39. MSRB, 30 June 1814.

40. Gregg, "War on Missouri Frontier," pp. 332-333.

41. MSRB, 31 December 1814.

42. Francis Bernard Heitman, *Historical Register and Dictionary of the United States Army*, 2 vols. (Washington, D.C.: Government Printing Office, 1903), 1:275.

43. Wesley, "James Callaway," p. 66; Gregg, "War on Missouri Frontier," p. 332.

44. Deposition of William Becknell, 4 May 1816, Maher Collection, Callaway Papers, Missouri Historical Society, St. Louis, Missouri.

45. The following account of Major Zachary Taylor's expedition and the Battle of Credit Island is an amalgamation of a letter and diary written by Callaway within hours of the events. These are found in Wesley, "James Callaway," pp. 69-71, 74-77.

46. Credit Island is now a park within the city limits of Davenport, Iowa. The retreat covered the distance between Davenport and Keokuk, Iowa. *Ibid.*, p. 69.

47. *Ibid.*, and accompanying map of "Fort Johnson, Drawn by Capt. Callaway."

48. Gregg, "War on Missouri Frontier," pp. 336-337.

49. Becknell's wife may have been dying or recently dead. MSRB, 30 September 1814.

50. Wesley, "James Callaway," pp. 71-72.

51. Gregg, "War on Missouri Frontier," p. 337.

52. *Ibid.*, p. 340.

53. William S. Bryan and Robert Rose, *A History of the Pioneer Families of Missouri* (St. Louis: Bryan, Brand and Company, 1876), p. 95.

54. Wesley, "James Callaway," p. 73.

55. St. Louis Missouri Gazette, 18 March 1815, p. 3.

56. Events surrounding the ambush of Callaway and his men are widely recounted and debated in Missouri histories; even the date of the

incident has been questioned. The ambush did indeed occur on March 7, but not on the same day as Callaway left Fort Clemson in pursuit of the stolen horses, as is generally believed. This is affirmed by Callaway's and Becknell's writings. The above summary of Callaway's ambush is drawn from: Wesley, "James Callaway," pp. 50-52, and Bryan, A *History of Pioneer Families*, p. 95.

57. Woods' Fort was on the modern site of Troy, Lincoln County, Missouri. Shoemaker, "Missouri Forts," p. 285; and MSRB, 20 June 1815.

58. Gregg, "War on Missouri Frontier," p. 342.

59. Homer De Golyer notes from St. Charles County Deed Records, Book C, p. 271, HDBC.

60. U.S. Department of Commerce, Bureau of the Census, *1850 Census Titus County, Texas*, (Washington, D.C., National Archives of the United States, Roll No. 915, n.d.). See also Homer De Golyer, "William Becknell," p. 52, HDBC.

61. Will of Mary Becknell.

62. Early activities at Boone's Lick are widely recounted in Missouri histories, but the Boone-Van Bibber episode of 1804 is not included. Homer De Golyer notes from an interview with Nathan Boone, n.d., n.p., Draper Notes, Wisconsin Historical Society, Madison, HDBC. See also, *Kansas City Times*, 30 August 1960, p. 5.

63. John Bradbury, *Travels in the Interior of America* (Liverpool: Sherwood, Neely, and Jones, 1817; reprinted, Ann Arbor, Michigan: University Microfilms, Inc., 1966), p. 25.

64. *History of Saline County, Missouri* (St. Louis: n.p., 1881; reprinted., St. Louis, Mo.: Missouri Historical Society, 1974), p. 475.

65. Homer De Golyer notes from Howard County Circuit Court Records, 30 December 1816, HDBC.

66. Robidoux was the eldest of six brothers involved in the fur trade. His roots were deep in Missouri and his friends were influential. Members of the first territorial House of Representatives of Missouri met officially in his St. Louis home in December, 1812, to elect several officers. David J. Weber, *The Taos Trappers* (Norman: University of Oklahoma Press, 1971), pp. 85-86. Court account found in Abiel Leonard Collection, "Abstract of Certain suits instituted and determined in the Howard circuit court in which Charles Lucas Esq. engaged as Attorney," State Historical Society of Missouri Manuscripts, collection number 1013, folder 83, Columbia, Missouri. See also Merrill J. Mattes, "Joseph Robidoux," in *The Mountain Men and the Fur Trade of the Far West*, ed. Leroy R. Hafen (Glendale: Arthur H. Clark, 1971), 8:294.

67. Charley Carr to John B. Callaway, 5 November 1817, Maher Collection, Callaway Papers, Missouri Historical Society, St. Louis, Missouri. HDBC.

68. Homer De Golyer notes from Howard County Deed Record Book B., p. 103, HDBC; and map of "The City of Franklin" in Abiel Leonard Collection, folder 622, State Historical Society of Missouri, Columbia, Missouri.

69. Homer De Golyer notes from Howard County Circuit Court Records, 11 November 1817, HDBC.

70. Violette, *History of Missouri*, p. 94.

71. Walter B. Stevens, *Centennial History of Missouri*, 5 vols. (St. Louis: S. J. Clarke Publishing Co., 1921), 1;13.

72. Missouri Historical Society Library, St. Louis, Howard County, Missouri 1817 Taxpayer, p. 79.

73. Williams, *Missouri, Mother of the West*, 1:116-117.

74. Homer De Golyer notes from Howard County Circuit Court Records, 6 June 1818; 10 June 1818; 16 June 1818. HDBC.

75. *St. Louis Missouri Gazette and Public Advertiser*, 2 October 1818, p. 3.

76. Ira Emmons owed thirty dollars to James Callaway during the war. Perhaps this is when Becknell and the Emmons brothers first met. Wesley, "James Callaway," p. 79. See also, Homer De Golyer's notes of "Becknell & Emmons" dealings with John Rawlins. HDBC.

77. *St. Louis Missouri Gazette and Public Advertiser*, 4 December 1818, p. 3.

78. *History of Saline County*, p. 475.

79. B. H. Reeves, "Money Expended and paid to Hands," 1825-1827, Abiel Leonard Collection, folder 57, State Historical Society of Missouri, Columbia, Missouri.

80. WPA Writer's Program, *Missouri* (New York: Hastings House Publishers, 1954), p. 353.

81. *Kansas City Times*, 30 August 1960, p. 5.

82. Floyd Shoemaker, ed., "Missouriana," *Missouri Historical Review* 27 (April 1933): pp. 270-271.

83. *Kansas City Times*, 30 August 1960, p. 5; and Shoemaker, "Missouriana," pp. 270-271.

84. Homer De Golyer notes from Howard County Circuit Court Records, 19 August 1819. HDBC.

85. *Franklin Missouri Intelligencer and Boon's Lick Advertiser*, 27 August 1819, p. 2.

86. The 1830 Census indicates Becknell had a daughter between ten and fourteen years old. U.S. Department of Commerce, Bureau of the Census, Fifth Census of the United States, 1830: Population vol. 2 (Washington, D.C.: National Archives of the United States, Record Group No. 29, Mo. roles 72-73, 1946), 2:232. Microfilm; and Walter B. Stevens, *Centennial History of Missouri*, 5 vols. (St. Louis: S. J. Clarke Publishing Co., 1921), 1:23.

87. *Franklin Missouri Intelligencer*, 7 January, 1820, p. 3.

88. Homer De Golyer notes from Howard County Deed Record Book E, p. 230. HDBC.

89. Homer De Golyer notes from Howard County Circuit Court Records, 29 May 1821; 28 July 1820.

90. Becknell had apparently been elected Captain in the militia sometime after 1815. *Franklin Missouri Intelligencer*, 29 July 1820, p. 2.

91. *Franklin Missouri Intelligencer*, 5 August 1820, p. 3.

92. *Franklin Missouri Intelligencer*, 9 September 1820, p. 3.

93. Violette, *History of Missouri*, pp. 142-143.

94. Homer De Golyer notes, "An Agreement Between Thomas A. Smith and William Becknell & Co.," 18 August 1821. HDBC.

95. Homer De Golyer notes from Howard County Circuit Court, 29 May 1821. HDBC.

Chapter II. On the Trail to Santa Fe

1. *Franklin Missouri Intelligencer*, 25 June 1821, p. 3.

2. *St. Louis Missouri Gazette & Public Advertiser*, 5 September 1821, p. 2.

3. Homer De Golyer notes, Homer De Golyer Becknell Collection, hereinafter HDBC.

4. *Franklin Missouri Intelligencer*, 14 August 1821, p. 3.

5. *Howard County Circuit Court Years 1816-1818*, vol. unknown, p. 88 (Salt Lake City: Genealogical Society of Salt Lake City, Ut., 1947) micorfilm Mo 1-145.

6. David J. Weber, *The Taos Trappers* (Norman: University of Oklahoma Press, 1971), p. 41.

7. *Ibid.*, pp. 41-45. Also, for a semi-fictionalized account of Williams' activities in the Far West see David H. Coyner, *The Lost Trappers*, ed. David J. Weber (Albuquerque: University of New Mexico Press, 1970).

8. R. L. Duffus, *The Santa Fe Trail* (New York: Tudor Publishing Co., 1930) pp. 91-92.

9. Weber, *Taos Trappers*, pp. 32-34.

10. Duffus, *Santa Fe Trail*, p. 38.

11. Julia K. Garrett, *Green Flag Over Texas* (New York: Cordova Press, 1939), p. 225.

12. Weber, *Taos Trappers*, p. 52.

13. Marc Simmons, "Opening the Santa Fe Trail," Westport Historical Quarterly, 7 (June 1971), pp. 3-7.

14. Weber, *Taos Trappers*, p. 35.

15. Kate L. Gregg, ed., *The Road to Santa Fe* (Albuquerque: University of New Mexico Press, 1952), p. 270.

16. Homer De Golyer notes from Howard County Circuit Court Records, 7 September 1821. HDBC.

17. Homer De Golyer notes from Howard County Circuit Court Records, 17 September 1821. HDBC.

18. *Franklin Missouri Intelligencer*, 22 January 1822, p. 4; 12 February 1822, p. 4.

19. *Howard County Circuit Years 1819-1823*, vol. 2, pp. 350, 367 (Salt Lake City: Genealogical Society of Salt Lake City, Ut., 1974) microfilm Mo 1-045.

20. Lane's suit also mentions $500 damages, but this sum is not referred to again in extant records. Homer De Golyer notes from Howard County Circuit Court Records, 8 November 1821. HDBC.

21. *Howard County Circuit Court Years 1819-1823*, vol. 2, pp. 389, 414-415 (Salt Lake City: Genealogical Society of Salt Lake City, Ut., 1974) microfilm Mo 1-045.

22. *Ibid.*, pp. 408, 429.

23. Most accounts agree that Becknell took only three or four men with him on his first journey to Santa Fe, while some place the total at between twenty and thirty. See, i.e., Gregg, *Road to Santa Fe*, p. 2; and Eugene Morrow Violette, *A History of Missouri* (Cape Girardeau: Ramfre Press, 1951), p. 190.

24. *Franklin Missouri Intelligencer*, 22 April 1823, p. 2. Other sources of this event are found in the *Missouri Historical Review* (1910), and Archer Butler Hulbert, *Southwest on the Turquoise Trail* (Denver: Stewart Commission of Colorado College and the Denver Public Library, 1933). All subsequent references provided by the *Franklin Missouri Intelligencer*.

25. I believe the journal of "Capt. William Becknell" is fairly accurate. Statements in the *Franklin Missouri Intelligencer* of 18 February 1823, and 22 April 1823, referred to in Chapter three indicate that Becknell provided substantial information for the journal. Seymour V. Connor and Jimmy M. Skaggs, *Broadcloth and Britches* (College Station: Texas A&M University Press, 1977), pp. 15-16.

26. *Ibid.*, See also David J. Weber, "William Becknell as a Mountain Man: Two Letters," *New Mexico Historical Review*, 46 (July 1971): pp. 255-256.

27. Josiah Gregg, *Commerce of the Prairies*, ed., Max L. Moorhead (Norman: University of Oklahoma Press, 1954), p. 13.

28. The basis for this interpretationis found in Simmons, "Opening the Santa Fe Trail," pp. 4-6.

29. *Franklin Missouri Intelligencer*, 9 October 1821, p. 1.

30. Gregg, *Road to Santa Fe*, pp. 1, 214-215.

31. *Ibid.*, pp. 214-215.

32. Hulbert, *Turquoise Trail*, p. 61.

33. Becknell was crossing Raton Pass. Duffus, *Santa Fe Trail*, p. 68.

34. Gregg, *Commerce of the Prairies*, ed., Moorhead, p. 13.

35. French was widely spoken in Missouri, a former part of French Louisiana, and portions of newspapers there were printed in French. See, e.g., *St. Louis Louisiana Gazette*, 3 May 1810; Weber, *Taos Trappers*, p. 52.

36. Connor and Skaggs, *Broadcloth*, p. 15.

37. Simmons, "Opening the Santa Fe Trail," pp. 3, 7; and Iris H. Wilson, *William Wolfskill* (Glendale: Arthur H. Clark Co., 1965), p. 36.

38. Becknell's comments were mild compared to those made by later Anglo-American visitors to New Mexico: Rufus B. Sage, "Degenerate Inhabitants of New Mexico," in *Foreigners in Their Native Land*, ed., David J. Weber (Albuquerque: University of New Mexico Press, 1973), pp. 71-75.

39. Weber, *Taos Trappers*, p. 54.

40. An undated map of Franklin shows lot fifty-six to be owned by "Rivill [?] and Harris," while lots fifty-two and fifty-three were owned by "Wm. Becknell." The three lots shared frontage on a street "66 ft. in width." "The City of Franklin," Abiel Leonard Collection, folder 622, State Historical Society of Missouri, Columbia, Missouri.

41. Duffus, *Santa Fe Trail*, pp. 68-69.

42. *Howard County Circuit Court Years 1819-1823*, vol. 2, p. 446 (Salt Lake City: Geneological Society of Salt Lake City, Utah, 1974) microfilm

Mo 1-045. Jesse Morrison and Thomas Hubbard appeared before Court Clerk Gray Bynum on March 27, 1822, and promised to pay Becknell's debt to Hardage Lane if Becknell could not do so. Homer De Golyer notes from Howard County Circuit Court Records, HDBC.

Chapter III. From Trail to Roadway

1. Robert L. Duffus, *The Santa Fe Trail* (Albuquerque: University of New Mexico, 1972 reprint), p. 69.

2. David J. Weber, *The Taos Trappers* (Norman: University of Oklahoma Press, 1971), p. 58; *Franklin Missouri Intelligencer*, 3 September 1822, p. 3; Duffus, *Santa Fe Trail*, p. 77.

3. Marc Simmons, "Opening the Santa Fe Trail," *Westport Historical Quarterly* 7 (June 1971), p. 6.

4. Josiah Gregg, *Commerce of the Prairies*, ed. Max L. Moorhead (Norman: University of Oklahoma Press, 1958), pp. 14-15.

5. *Ibid.*, p. 15.

6. Josiah Gregg, *Diary and Letters of Josiah Gregg*, ed. Maurice Garland Fulton, 2 vols. (Norman: University of Oklahoma, 1941), I:86.

7. Simmons, "Opening the Santa Fe Trail," pp. 258-259.

8. Gregg described Becknell's farm, but gave no indication of talking to his former neighbor. It should also be remembered that Gregg might have quoted Becknell on the subject had he been the source of such information. Gregg, *Diary and Letters*, I:86. For Gregg's errors see Josiah Gregg, *Commerce of the Prairies*, ed. Moorhead, p. 15.

9. Duffus, *Santa Fe Trail*, p. 79. See, also, Iris H. Wilson, *William Wolfskill* (Glendale, Arthur H. Clark Co., 1965), p. 38.

10. Weber, *Taos Trappers*, p. 58.

11. Alphonso Wetmore wrote on August 19, 1824, that Becknell "took with him a wagon, as did two or three of his associates." Augustus Storrs and Alphonso Wetmore, *Santa Fe Trail First Reports: 1825* (Houston: Stagecoach Press, 1960), p. 61.

12. *Franklin Missouri Intelligencer*, 13 February, 1823, p. 3.

13. *Franklin Missouri Intelligencer*, 13 February 1823, p. 3.

14. *Franklin Missouri Intelligencer*, 3 October 1822, p. 2.

15. *Howard County Circuit Court Years 1819-1823*, vol. 2, pp. 458, 475-476 (Salt Lake City: Geneological Society of Salt Lake City, Utah, 1974) microfilm Mo 1-045.

16. *Ibid.*, pp. 478-479.

17. *Ibid.*, pp. 457, 479.

18. *Ibid.*, p. 511.

19. *Ibid., p. 531.*

20. *Franklin Missouri Intelligencer*, 18 February 1823, p. 3.

21. Notices of letters for Becknell were published in the *Franklin Missouri Intelligencer* on the following dates: 1 July 1823, p. 3; 30 September 1823, p. 3, and 10 July 1824, p. 3.

22. Letter from Alphonso Wetmore to Congressman John Scott, August 19, 1824, in Augustus Storrs and Alphonso Wetmore, *Santa Fe Trail First Reports: 1825* (Houston: Stagecoach Press, 1960), p. 68.

23. Weber, *Taos Trappers*, p. 78.

24. David J. Weber, "William Becknell as a Mountain Man: Two Letters," *New Mexico Historical Review* 46 (July 1971), p. 253.

25. Weber, *Taos Trappers*, p. 78.

26. *Ibid.*, p. 79.

27. Weber, "Becknell as a Mountain Man," p. 255.

28. See Carl I. Wheat, *Mapping the Transmississippi West*, 5 vols. (San Francisco: Institute of Historical Cartography, 1957), 2.

29. Weber, "Becknell as a Mountain Man," p. 256.

30. Significantly, Becknell's party consisted of employees rather than independent companions as on his first and perhaps second visits to New Mexico. He may have numbered among his employees native New Mexicans. *Ibid.*, p. 254. All subsequent references to this article found in *Franklin Missouri Intelligencer*, 25 June 1825, p. 3.

31. Weber, *Taos Trappers*, p. 79.

32. Weber, "Becknell as a Mountain Man," p. 254.

33. *Franklin Missouri Intelligencer*, 25 June 1825, p. 3.

34. Weber, "Becknell as a Mountain Man," p. 254.

35. "It is reported that Col. Cooper's party were robbed by the Indians, and left in a starving condition." *Franklin Missouri Intelligencer*, 3 September 1822, p. 3. "The arrival of the greater part of the company under the superintendence of Col. Cooper from Santa Fe happily contradicts the report afloat a few weeks since, of their having been 'robbed and left in a starving condition.'" *Franklin Missouri Intelligencer*, 8 October 1822, p. 3.

36. Weber, "Becknell as a Mountain Man," p. 260. See also, e.g., *Franklin Missouri Intelligencer*, 25 June 1825, p. 3.

37. William H. Goetzmann, "The Mountain Man as Jackson Man," *American Quarterly* 15 (Fall 1963), p. 405.

38. Storrs and Wetmore, *First Reports*, pp. 61-68.

39. *Ibid.*, pp. 55-57, p. 49.

40. *Ibid.*, p. 16.

41. Duffus, *Santa Fe Trail*, p. 85.

42. B. H. Reeves, "No. 1 B. H. Reeves," 8 July 1825, Abiel Leonard Collection, folder 57, State Historical Society of Missouri, Columbia, Missouri.

43. B. H. Reeves, "Money Expended & paid to Hands," 1825-1827, Abiel Leonard Collection folder 57, State Historical Society of Missouri, Columbia, Missouri.

44. B. H. Reeves, "Memorandum of days necessarily employed as commissioner of the Mexican Road," Abiel Leonard Collection, folder 57, State Historical Society of Missouri, Columbia, Missouri.

45. B. H. Reeves, "Money Expended & paid to Hands," 1825-1827, Abiel Leonard Collection, folder 57, State Historical Society of Missouri, Columbia, Missouri.

46. B. H. Reeves, "In Account Current With the Mexican Road Commissioners," no date, Abiel Leonard Collection, folder 64, State Historical Society of Missouri, Columbia, Missouri.

47. B. H. Reeves, "The Mexican Road Commission," 21 January 1826, Abiel Leonard Collection, folder 59, State Historical Society, Columbia, Missouri.

48. Reeves' records state that on "Monday 10th Octr 1825" the company camped to repair "the tire of one wheel" which was done "by putting on a tire of raw Buffaloe [*sic*] hide," and that "this creek nuosho [*sic*] on which we are encamped empties into the Arkansas River one or two miles below the mouth of the Verdigris as we are informed by Captains Cooper & Becknal [*sic*]." B. H. Reeves, "Journal," 1825, Abiel Leonard Collection, folder 58, State Historical Society of Missouri, Columbia, Missouri. Notebook [by Davis?] Davis Collection, State Historical Society of Missouri, Columbia, Missouri.

49. B. H. Reeves, "Journal," 12 October 1825, Abiel Leonard Collection, folder 58, State Historical Society, Columbia, Missouri.

50. Notebook [by Davis ?], Davis Collection, State Historical Society, Columbia, Missouri.

51. B. H. Reeves, "Journal," 21 October 1825, Abiel Leonard Collection, folder 58, State Historical Society, Columbia, Missouri.

52. This is the last indication of Becknell's employment found in Reeves' records. Henry E. Dever and James Bradley entered suit against Becknell in Howard County Court during the February term, 1826. The

case continued through the October term, and I could not discover its outcome. Howard County Circuit Court Record, vol. 3, pp. 258, 310, 367
(Salt Lake City: Geneological Society of Salt Lake City, Utah, 1947)
microfilm Mo 1-045.

Chapter IV. Becknell's Public Service

1. Lyn McDaniel, ed., *Bicentennial Boonslick History* (n.p.:
Boonslick Historical Society, 1976), p. 50.

2. Deed Books A and B, Saline County, Missouri, 1821-28, p. 102;
Archer Butler Hulbert, *Southwest on the Turquoise Trail* (Denver: The
Stewart Commission of Colorado College and The Denver Public
Library, 1933), p. 69.

3. McDaniel, *Boonslick History*, pp. 45, 50.

4. *Ibid.*, p. 45.

5. B. H. Reeves, "In Account Current With the Mexican Road Commissioners," no date, Abiel Leonard Collection, folder 64, State Historical
Society of Missouri, Columbia, Missouri.

6. Deed Book A and B, Saline County, Missouri, 1821-28, p. 102.

7. *Ibid.; St. Louis Missouri Republican*, 2 December, 1828, p. 3;
Homer De Golyer notes from "The Journal of the 1st Session of the 5th
General Assembly of the State of Missouri," pp. 194-195. HDBC.

8. William Becknell to Mr. A. W. Payne, or Brother, 4 April, 1829,
M. U. Payne Papers, State Historical Society of Missouri, Columbia,
Missouri.

9. Homer De Golyer notes from the Sappington Papers, 1828-1831,
Missouri Historical Society, St. Louis, Missouri. HDBC.

10. *Ibid.*

11. U.S. Department of Commerce, Bureau of the Census, Fifth Census of the United States, 1830: Population, vol. 2 (Washington, D.C.: National Archives of the United States, Record Group No. 29, Mo. rolls
72-73, 1946), 2:232. Microfilm. See Will of Mary Becknell, Book B, Red
River County Court House, Texas, p. 61.

12. John Vulmer Mering, *The Whig Party in Missouri* (Columbia:
University of Missouri Press, 1967), p. 19; *Fayette Missouri Intelligencer*,
14 August 1830, p. 3.

13. Homer De Golyer notes from "The Journal of the House of Representatives of the State of Missouri 1st Session of the 6th General Assembly, opening November 15th, 1830," p. 86. HDBC.

14. William Becknell to John Sappington, 24 December 1830, Sappington Collection, State Historical Society of Missouri, Columbia, Missouri.

15. Homer De Golyer notes from Sappington Papers, 1828-1831, Missouri Historical Society, St. Louis, Missouri. HDBC.

16. McDaniel, *Boonslick History*, p. 52.

17. U.S. Department of Commerce, Bureau of the Census, Fifth Census of the United States, 1830: Population, vol. 2:234.

18. McDaniel, *Boonslick History*, p. 52.

19. An indication of Marmaduke's affiliation with the Sappington family is revealed in Marmaduke's journal of Augustus Storrs' Santa Fe expedition, when he records that we "Crossed the Missouri river at Hardiman's ferry (Arrow Rock) six miles above Franklin, on Sunday the 16th May, 1824, and encamped two miles from the ferry, in a beautiful prairie (Sappington settlement)." Hulbert, *Turquoise Trail*, p. 69.

20. History of Saline County, Missouri (St. Louis: n.p., 1881; reprinted, St. Louis, Missouri: Missouri Historical Society, 1974), p. 216.

21. *Ibid.*, pp. 216-217.

22. *Ibid.*

23. Book G. Saline County, Missouri, pp. 220-221.

24. Jesse Nave bill of sale to William Becknell and Transfer to John Becknell, Deed Book C, Red River County Court House, Texas, p. 474. HDBC.

25. Will of Mary Becknell, Book B, Red River County Court House, Texas, p. 61. See also, "Martin Becknall, Phillis Becknall vs. B. H. Epperson," Estate Papers of Mary Becknell, 1862-1864, 995 vol. 17 No. 477, State Historical Society of Missouri, Columbia, Missouri.

26. Homer De Golyer notes from Cooper County Court Records, 14 June 1834. HDBC; William Becknell to Sam Houston, 28 May 1836, Thomas Jefferson Green Papers, Southern Historical Collection, University of North Carolina, Chapel Hill, North Carolina. Copy obtained from Rex W. Strickland, El Paso, Texas; and Josiah Gregg, *Diary and Letters of Josiah Gregg*, ed. Maurice Garland Fulton, 2 vols. (Norman: University of Oklahoma, 1941), I, 86.

Chapter V. Becknell Settles in Texas

1. William Becknell to Sam Houston, 28 May 1836, Thomas Jefferson Green Papers, Southern Historical Collection, University of North Carolina, Chapel Hill, North Carolina. See also, Walter Prescott Webb, ed., *The Handbook of Texas*, 3 vols. (Austin: Texas State Historical Association, 1952), 1:134.

2. Rupert Norval Richardson, Ernest Wallace, and Adrian N. Anderson, *Texas the Lone Star State* (Englewood Cliffs, New Jersey: Prentice Hall, Inc., 1970), p. 54.

3. Ibid., pp. 53-55.

4. Ibid., pp. 59, 78-79.

5. The above summary of Texas Revolution events is drawn from Richardson, *Texas*, pp. 82-98.

6. Pat B. Clark, *The History of Clarksville and Old Red River County* (Dallas: Mathis, Van Nort and Company, 1937), pp. 14-15.

7. Clark's account of Crockett's visit to the area contains several errors. He states that Crockett's tour occurred during the "summer of 1835," when Crockett did not leave Tennessee for Texas until November, 1835. That Crockett and Becknell were friends has no apparent basis in historical record, although Crockett may have been an admirer of Becknell's accomplishments and therefore desirous of meeting him. Another version of Clark's story is found in James Atkins Shackford, *David Crockett, The Man and the Legend* (Austin: Pemberton Press, 1968), p. 215.

8. Homer De Golyer notes from Executive Letter Book No. 35, pp. 67-68. HDBC.

9. Becknell to Houston, 28 May 1836, T. J. Green Papers.

10. "A Master Rold [sic] and inspection Returne [sic] of a Company of Mounted Volunteers, Raised and Organized, 25, Miles South of Red River," 28 April 1836, T. J. Green Papers.

11. Becknell to Houston, 28 May 1836, T. J. Green Papers.

12. Thomas Jefferson Green to William Becknell, 25 June 1836, T. J. Green Papers. Typescript HDBC. Green, a recent arrival from the United States, was leader of "a group of disgruntled and ambitious army officers" opposed to the government's plan to release the captured Santa Anna as a provision forced President Burnet to remove Santa Anna and his entourage from the Texas warship Invincible, rather than let the hated dictator sail to freedom. The army's lack of cooperation with the government

was a serious threat to the survival of the Republic of Texas during its early months. Richardson, *Texas*, p. 99.

13. This enumeration of the Red River Blues and the following account of their journey to Lavaca Bay is, except where noted, compiled from "Descriptive Muster Roll of Captain Becknell's Company Mustered into service on the 14th of July 1836 at James Clark's Sulphurfork Prairie," and "Report of Capt Becknal's [*sic*] company of mounted rangers, called the Red River Blues August 26th 1836," both in T. J. Green Papers.

14. Rex W. Strickland, "Anglo-American Activities in Northeastern Texas" (Ph.D. dissertation, University of Texas, 1937), pp. 262-263.

15. Two William Coopers were original members of Stephen Austin's colony. To avoid confusion, neighbors dubbed them "Cow" and "Sawmill," based upon their differing occupations: "Cow" Cooper had a ranch east of the Brazos, south of San Felipe. Webb, *Handbook*, 1:408.

16. These units were commanded by Captains William H. Smith and John Hart. Ibid., pp. 262-265, 268; *Columbia Telegraph and Texas Register*, 11 October 1836, p. 3.

17. Becknell's eastward tangent from the deserted village of Victoria to Dimmitt's Landing on the Lavaca River was a result of the general redeployment of Texas forces from Coleto Creek, ten miles southwest of Victoria, to encampments in the vicinity of Dimmitt's supply station on the Lavaca River. Camp Johnson was five miles down river from Dimmitt's Landing. Approximately 2,500 troops, Texans and recently-arrived volunteers from the United States were stationed in the area. Gerald S. Pierce, *Texas Under Arms* (Austin: Encino Press, 1969), pp. 32, 43-44, 79, 159-160, 168-169.

18. Thomas Jefferson Green to William Becknell, 7 September 1836, [T. J. Green Papers ?], typescript HDBC.

19. William Becknell to Thomas Jefferson Green, 13 September 1836, T. J. Green Papers. Copy obtained from Rex W. Strickland, El Paso, Texas. Becknell's detachment evidently traveled fifty miles up the Lavaca River to the vicinity of present-day Hallettsville, founded in 1836 on land given by Mrs. John Hallett [Hallet]. Webb, *Handbook*, 1:758.

20. Edgar B. Wesley, "James Callaway in the War of 1812; Letters, Diary, and Rosters, "Missouri Historical Collections, 5 (October 1827): 77, 78, 81; Floyd C. Shoemaker, ed., "Missouri Forts in the War of 1812," *Missouri Historical Review* 26 (April 1932): 286-287; Webb, *Texas*, 1:465, 951.

21. Strickland, "Anglo-American Activities," pp. 268, 270.

22. Ibid., pp. 265, 268, 276-277; "Descriptive Muster Roll of Captain Becknell's Company, Mustered into Service on the 14th of July 1836 at James Clark's Sulphurfork Prairie," T. J. Green Papers; Webb, *Handbook*, 2:938.

23. Ibid., p. 276.

24. *Columbia Telegraph and Texas Register*, 11 October 1836, pp. 2, 3.

25. Strickland, "Anglo-American Activities," pp. 277, 270.

26. Ibid., p. 277.

27. Ibid., pp. 277-278.

28. *Columbia Telegraph and Texas Register*, 25 October 1836, p. 1.

29. Strickland, "Anglo-American Activities," p. 263.

30. Seymour V. Connor, ed., *Texas Treasury Papers*, 4 vols. (Austin: Texas State Library, 1955), 1:1-3.

31. Muster Roll Book of the General Land Office, Soldiers of the Republic of Texas Part III. (Austin: General Land Office: 1957), p. 241.

32. William Becknell to Thomas Jefferson Green, 18 October 1836, HDBC [T. J. Green Papers ?].

33. Reasons for the marked contrast between Becknell's two letters to Green during the journey to the Red River settlements can only be surmised, but, again, Becknell's comments may have been couched in the prose of a more literate advisor at Nacogdoches. William Becknell to Thomas Jefferson Green, 4 October [November ?], 1836, HDBC, [T. J. Green Papers ?].

34. General Green, who as a resident of Florida before the revolution had speculated in land on the Sulphur Fork and other parts of Texas, was concerned with fostering acceptance by the Congress of the Texas Rail-Road Navigation and Banking Company — "a sort of Credit Mobilier" that sought control of transportation and banking in the infant republic — in which he was a stockholder. This and other concerns may explain why Becknell's expedition never materialized. William Ransom Hogan, *The Texas Republic* (Austin: University of Texas Press, 1946), pp. 85, 97; Richardson, *Texas*, p. 107; Webb, *Handbook*, 1:165.

35. W. W. Newcomb, Jr., *The Indians of Texas* (Austin: University of Texas Press, 1978), p. 347.

36. Strickland, "Anglo-American Activities," pp. 320-321.

37. Pierce, *Texas Under Arms*, pp. 30-31, 97-98, 157.

38. Biographical and Historical Notes, Texas State Archives, Texas State Library, typescript HDBC.

39. Pierce, *Texas Under Arms*, pp. 19, 78, 97-99, 156-158; Strickland, "Anglo-American Activities," pp. 329-340.

40. "Red River County Tax Rolls 1838-1910," 1:2.

41. Book C, Red River County Court House, Texas, pp. 13, 96, 337.

42. Gifford White, ed., *The 1840 Census of the Republic of Texas* (Austin: Pemberton Press, 1966), p. 138.

43. "Red River County Tax Rolls 1838-1910," 3;3, 4:2.

44. Book A, Red River District Court, Red River Court House, Texas, pp. 7, 30.

45. Becknell served seventy-five days in 1841, and fifteen days in 1842. John C. Becknell served sixty-three days in 1841, and fifteen days in 1842. Notes found in HDBC [Red River County Records ?], William Becknell, William Becknell [Jr.,], and John Becknell sworn statement 2 December 1849, Red River County, Texas.

46. Becknell also owned 1,030 acres in Lamar County, west of Red River County. "Red River County Tax Rolls 1838-1910," 6:2.

47. John Sappington Papers, January 1830-March 1831, Correspondence and Papers, State Historical Society of Missouri, Columbia, Missouri, folders 2, 18, 20, 22, 94.

48. Lyn McDaniel, ed., *Bicentennial Boonslick History* (n.p.: Boonslick Historical Society, 1976), p. 53.

49. Sappington Papers, folder 22; The Marmaduke Papers contain a sign printed by the Vicksburg Whig advertising "Doctor John Sappington's Anti Fever and Ague Pills for Sale at Price Reduced." M. M. Marmaduke Collection, State Historical Society of Missouri, Columbia, Missouri, folder 1.

50. William Becknell, "Deposition," 1853, Typescript Collection, State Historical Society of Missouri, Columbia, Missouri, folder 478; Eugene W. Bowers and Evelyn Oppenheimer, *Red River Dust* (Waco: Word Books, 1968), pp. 53-55.

51. Sappington's papers include this entry: "Septr. 28th 1835 Rcd of Dr. Sappington Twenty Five Dollars and 32 cents in full payment for my first trip in distributing his medicine. Peter Ringo." A similar statement dated November 7, 1835 is in the same folder. John Sappington Papers, January-December 1835, Correspondence and Papers, State Historical Society of Missouri, Columbia, Missouri, folder 22.

52. M. M. Marmaduke Collection, State Historical Society of Missouri, Columbia, Missouri, folder 13.

53. Richardson, *Texas*, p. 113.

54. Marmaduke and Becknell were apparently active in the medicine business as late as 1845. M. M. Marmaduke to William Becknell, November 15, 1845, n.p., authorizing Becknell to represent him in a business transaction in New Orleans. M. M. Marmaduke Papers, State Historical Society of Missouri, Columbia, Missouri, folder 16; Bowers, *Red River Dust*, p. 54; Becknell, "Deposition."

55. Becknell, "Deposition."

56. Bowers, *Red River Dust*, pp. 53, 55; Becknell, "Deposition"; Bowers, *Red River Dust*, p. 55.

57. Thomas B. Hall, "John Sappington." *Missouri Historical Review* 24 (January 1930): p. 198.

58. E. W. Bowers, "Appraisal of the Estate of William Becknell," 26 January 1857; Bowers, "Even-Handed Justice," 12 December 1955, both Typescript Collection, folder 477, State Historical Society of Missouri, Columbia, Missouri.

59. "Red River County Tax Rolls 1838-1910." Texas State Library Archives Division, Austin, Texas, 6:2, 7:2, 8:27; Red River County Texas, Record of Marks and Brands, 17 July 1848, No. 42. HDBC.

60. William Becknell to Thomas Jefferson Rusk, 17 September 1849, typescript, HDBC.

61. *1850 Census Titus County, Texas*, (Washington, D.C., National Archives of the United States, Roll No. 915, _____); John Becknell owned 1476 acres in Red River and Titus Counties, "on Sulphur fork." He was also involved in the migration of French Fourierites to Texas, dealing with "Mons. Cabet Chief man of the Icarian French now settled at Nauvoo in the State of Illinois. . . ." William A. Bicknell [*sic*] owned 1,476 acres in Red River County "near Old Choctaw Village." Comptroller of the State of Texas, *Abstract of Land Claims* (Galveston: Civilian Book Office, 1852), p. 399; Red River County Court Records, Clarksville, Texas, Book I, pp. 27, 44; Book J, p. 457. See also, Webb, *Handbook*, 1:873.

62. *Clarksville Standard*, 18 March 1854, p. 2.

63. *Clarksville Northern Standard*, 28 February 1852, p. 1.

64. *Clarksville Northern Standard*, 21 August 1852, p. 4.

65. *Clarksville Northern Standard*, 16 October 1852, p. 3; *Austin Texas State Gazette*, 5 March 1853, p. 1; *Clarksville Standard*, 31 December 1853, p. 4.

66. John Burlage and J. B. Hollingsworth, *Abstract of Valid Land Claims Compiled from the Records of the General Land Office and Court*

Claims of the State of Texas (Austin: John Marshall and Co., 1859), pp. 32, 68, 70-71.

67. Clarksville Northern Standard, 2 August 1845, p. 2; 18 March 1846, p. 3.

68. No extant information indicates that William Becknell ever visited California, although he knew at least one early settler, William Wolfskill. *Clarksville Standard*, 26 April 1856, p. 2. Becknell's great-great-grand-daughter has stated that "Capt. Bill was said to have died in his sleep. . . ." Mrs. Robert Short, Jr. to Texas Historical Survey Committee, 16 November 1957, personal files of Rex W. Strickland, El Paso, Texas.

69. There is some question as to whether William Becknell was "not of a religious turn of mind," at least in his later years. His wife was apparently a devout Methodist and left $500 "to assist in building a meeting house which is to be built near the grave [Becknell's] on the land which I have deeded to the Methodist Church." Will of Mary Becknell, Book B, Red River County Court House, Texas, p. 61. *History of Saline County, Missouri* (St. Louis: n.p., 1881; reprint ed., St. Louis, Missouri: Missouri Historical Society, 1974), pp. 216-217.

70. Bowers, "Appraisal of the Estate of William Becknell."

71. William Becknell died on April 25, 1856; the *Clarksville Standard* announced his death on April 26. Will of Mary Becknell.

72. William A. Becknell, Jr. was fatally "thrown from his horse against a tree" in 1858. John C. Becknell left Red River County sometime prior to 1862, and died in Mariposa County, California, sometime after 1884. Cornelia [Cornealia] Becknell Collins died prior to February, 1871. Mrs. Robert Short to Texas Historical Survey Committee, 16 November 1957; E. W. Bowers, "Correspondence attempting to locate Grave of William Becknell and other Becknell information," February 1955, Typescript Collection, folder 480; and E. W. Bowers, "Estate Papers of Mary Becknell," 12 December 1955, Typescript Collection, folder 477, both State Historical Society of Missouri, Columbia, Missouri.

73. The inscription reads, "William Becknell. Born in Virginia 1797. Pioneered the Santa Fe Trail. Served in the Army of the Republic of Texas, Died 1865." Both dates are incorrect.

TEXAS WESTERN PRESS

*gratefully acknowledges
the following endowments:*

THE MARY HANNER REDFORD MEMORIAL FUND
THE JUDGE AND MRS. ROBERT E. CUNNINGHAM FUND
THE DR. C. L. SONNICHSEN SOUTHWESTERN PUBLICATION FUND

*all of which make possible
this and other issues of*

SOUTHWESTERN STUDIES